BLACK GIRL BLISS

# Pussy Prayers

SACRED AND SENSUAL RITUALS
FOR WILD WOMEN OF COLOR

Pussy Prayers

**Eleven25 Media**
www.eleven25media.com

This book is written to set you on the journey to
sacred and sensual empowerment. This book does
not provide any medical advice or treatment of
medical or emotional issues. Use of the techniques
outlined in this book assumes personal
responsibility on behalf of the reader/practitioner,
not on the author or publisher.

2nd Edition, October 2018

## Dedication

For every black, brown, mixed, freckled,
hued, tea-stained, sun-kissed, magical,
melanin-filled, midnight-skinned, brown
brass, red clay colored woman — past,
present, and future, across all places,
spaces, times, and dimensions:

May we always be a reflection of divinity.

May we remember our beauty, our worth,
and our power.

And may we always pray with
— and for — our pussies.

Pussy Prayers

# Contents

Pussy Prayers

**-PART TWO-**

PART ONE

CHAPTER ONE

# I
# Start Here

*Pussy. Pussy. Pussy.*

How does this word make you feel?
Are you turned-on? Intrigued? Irritated?
Downright disgusted?

All these feelings are valid, so it's
better to get these things out in the open
here at the beginning, rather than to
realize halfway through the book that this
isn't for you.

*Pussy*. This is the term I will be using to refer to the creative space between your thighs. You might call it yoni, coochie, cookie, box, cat, #WetWet, #GoodGood, womb, or vagina (though that's only part of what's there). You might even have given her a woman's name, like Janet (*Ms. Jackson, if you're nasty*). I like using the word pussy.

Why? Because it's a "bad" word. It's irreverent. It's "unladylike." It's shocking. But the use of the word pussy is not vulgarity for vulgarity's sake. Words we've been taught are bad or naughty or nasty are usually words that carry tremendous power. Whether that power is positive or negative is for you to decide. These types of words capture your attention immediately (it made you decide to read this book, didn't it?) and regardless of how you feel about the word, you typically remember exactly what was said.

## On Using "Bad" Words

So-called "foul language" does something to our brains that makes us perk up. When it comes out of our mouths, it is usually emphatic. It makes a point clear, leaving no room for doubt about exactly what you meant. Admit it: when you use a word that has this kind of power, it feels good. Naughty. Sexy. It makes you and other people giggle, smirk, or blush. That sexy, powerful feeling is what we're after. That feeling should be the way we walk through our daily lives, standing in our feminine power and creating lives that bring us more of what we want.

I'll be using the word "pussy" to describe not only the entire physical vulvovaginal area (including the pubic mound, labia, clitoris, urethra, and vagina), but to include the space within yourself from which manifestations are conjured and birthed. I will try my best to refrain from using the term "womb" simply because a) not everyone has one and b) it has connotations of the physical birth of a child which is not exactly what we're discussing here.

## What You'll Learn Here

In this book, you will learn to harness your innate divinity, your holy femininity, through the positive attention, praise, and reverence of your pussy. You will begin to understand the historic perpetuation of

11

shame and negligence of your body.
Through this text, you will begin the
reclamation of your body through
powerful intention and learn how
connecting to the universal Divine
Feminine will help you to lead a juicy,
delicious life of pleasure.

This feminine power is what gives us
the confidence and charm to ease our way
into everything we desire. It is also the
power that allows us to love ourselves,
love other women, and allow other
women to lavish their love upon us. (If
you are or have been one of those women
who claim that they can't have female
friends, don't trust other women, etc.,
then this is for you.) This power allows us
to know ourselves intimately so that we
can share ourselves with another, and also
know when we should absolutely stay

away from something that is not good for us. This is about letting go of negative energy towards femininity and letting the energy from your true center direct your thoughts and actions.

I will share my own stories and experiences in this book in hopes that you find resonance, relief, and much-needed laughter around topics that can often be heavy, traumatic, or depressing. As a creator of spaces and content that center on spirituality, sexuality, and self-care, and also as someone who is self-taught about her body or her feminine power, it is my mission to curate and deliver this divine knowledge so that anyone who comes across this book, my websites, or attends any of my events walks away enchanted and transformed, fully committed to themselves and their pleasure, and more deeply connected to the sacred, sensual *knowing* inside all of us. We are sisters, creators, magical juju mamas entitled to – literally wired for – pleasure. We conceive and give birth through acts that center pleasure. We can use this same power of pleasure to manifest and give birth to whatever we desire. Creating, maintaining, and prioritizing our pleasure is the game-changer. It is required to achieve our highest feminine potential. Whether you believe it yet or not, you deserve pleasure, you are allowed pleasure, and by the end of this book, I hope that you understand how to curate and cultivate pleasure in every aspect of your life.

## Things to Note

You are not required to read this book in order. This book can be used as a reference guide, allowing you to flip over to any section and find what you need. If you really want to have fun, try opening this book to any page without looking and see what comes up. You may find that you have landed on precisely the information you need. However, if you skip straight to doing rituals and affirmations without addressing underlying issues, laying a strong foundation, and doing the inner work, you may not see the results you desire.

The first five chapters of this book will end with *Pleasure Principles* – a quick, bullet-point summary of major lessons from the chapter. If you choose not to read this book from beginning to end, you can always skim through the Pleasure Principles to get the gist of what you missed. There is no need to overwhelm or inundate yourself with information. Ideas will be repeated across chapters for emphasis and as reminders, so don't think that you'll miss anything by not reading this book cover to cover. Let yourself be divinely guided to where you need to be.

Pussy Prayers was written for Black women because throughout time and across the African diaspora, we have been forced to disconnect from our bodies for survival. While I'm sure that any person with a vagina could find this book useful and is welcome to take what they can from it (just like Black women have had to do each time we venture into the all-white self-help, personal development, and pleasure education spaces), this book covers common experiences and practices unique to the Black feminine experience. The language used in this book will be most familiar to Black women because I have written this in the same tone in which I would talk to a friend or sister. This is not discriminatory nor is it exclusive. It is, simply, unapologetically specific. This book is for all Black women, of all ages, of all backgrounds, and all beliefs. This is a safe space.

Please remember that your divine right to exist in a constant state of pleasure does not mean that you do not or should not feel the entire range of emotions. One of the most magical parts of womanhood is the way we can move about the emotional spectrum at a moment's notice. People out of tune with our true nature will call us "erratic" or "crazy" when really, we're just as natural as the wind, the water, and the earth. All of nature's elements present aspects of beauty, elegance, purity, and peace. Nature's elements also present aspects of chaos, fury, barrenness, coldness, and destruction. We are made of the same atoms that make up earth and stars, and therefore are capable of all of their attributes. These emotions are natural, and they feel *damn* good when we get to express them the way we want. Even in these moments, we find a way back to pleasure.

Another thing to note about this book is that at times it will refer to sexual abuse and trauma. I encourage anyone who has a history of these experiences to seek professional help in the ways that best help you to process these events. This book will provide personal and spiritual practices that you can take part in, but they should not be used to replace therapy and spiritual counseling if these experiences cause overwhelming or debilitating and harmful mental and emotional responses.

This book provides a natural, holistic, physical, and spiritual approach to feminine wellness. This book will not diagnose or treat any physical ailments. It will not discourage you from seeking professional help (medical, psychological, and otherwise) as needed. It will, however, inspire you to do whatever it is you need to restore yourself.

This book is an introduction, not an encyclopedia. This journey will require you to do your own research, find your teachers, and allow yourself to be led to correct information that resonates with you. This book is only one part of what you'll need. This is your jump start, the kick in the ass you might need to reclaim control of your life and your destiny.

Many women may come to this book looking for tips and tricks to sex or sex magic and manifestation. All of that is here, but what takes priority over that is making sure that you are on your way to becoming or restoring the woman you need to be in order to engage in healthy sexual experiences, manifest for your highest good, and understand just how much power you're packing. This is not to be underestimated. Did you have a mother, aunt, or granny that would need to wash dishes and clean the kitchen before she could start cooking? This is something like that. We need to clean you up and put things back in their proper places before we turn on the fire and start making magic happen. Here, you will learn — or remember — your way around the "kitchen" before you start making a six-course gourmet brunch, understand? Good.

**Rethink Womanhood**

This book will reorganize and redefine the way you express and experience your womanhood. Through the reclamation of your pussy, the divine portal through which all manifestations are birthed, you will learn how to truly connect with that which you desire. You will learn and develop the tools you need to create a life around your dreams and your passions, as

opposed to impositions and obligations.
This might feel strange, since we have not
let our innate and most passionate desires
run the show since we were small
children. We're out of practice. At times,
this book may conjure up feelings of
shame, doubt, and anxiety. Some of this
work may feel frivolous, even
irresponsible. That's okay. Please do not
beat yourself up over this. These feelings
are not your fault. They are the fault of
the patriarchal, capitalist, and generally
toxic society in which we were taught
what it meant to be a woman.

The patriarchy exists because of the
immaturity of men and the fragility of the
male ego. So many women, past and
present, have been taught to dim their
light to allow their man to shine, while
suffering abuse and being made to feel

incompetent by men inconvenienced and intimidated by feminine brilliance. Women globally have taken on the sexist and patriarchal values upheld across societies, and unlearning these values takes time and patience. When these negative feelings come up for you, remind yourself of your true nature, your divine birthright, and your Goddess-given power to get you back on track.

Over the course of this book, or as you flip back and forth at your leisure, I would like you to consider what I call *Pressure Points* – questions that tend to evoke a range of emotional responses depending on where you are in your relationship with the divine feminine and your own pussy. Take a moment to jot down your responses to these questions in a journal, in the Notes app on your phone,

or in a document on your computer —
anywhere that will allow these responses
to be kept private and accessible for you
to view and update as you move through
the book. By the end, you should be able
to see your progress through reviewing
your entries. For additional exercises and
resources to aid you on this journey, visit
Part Two of this book.

## Pressure Points

- Who taught you about what it meant to be a woman? When did you learn it and how did it make you feel about womanhood?
- What is "feminine" in your own words? Do you feel feminine? Why or why not?
- Do you enjoy being a woman? Have you always enjoyed womanhood? Explain.
- Is there a presence of divine femininity in your life, whether through your own personal spiritual practice or an organized religion? How does this feminine presence (or lack thereof) influence your ideas of femininity and womanhood?

Notice that these Pressure Points are spiritual in nature. That is because the way

Pussy Prayers

that you understand spirituality and
divinity directly impact the way that you
understand yourself. Thousands of years
ago, when pussies were revered as holy
and women were honored as oracles,
priestesses, healers, and goddesses, you
can imagine the impact that had on girls
coming into womanhood in those
societies. Women were seen as powerful,
as essential, as divine beings to be
worshipped. Conversely, once indigenous
matriarchal and goddess traditions were
criminalized and replaced with patriarchal
religions, you can imagine what happens
to a girl who is raised to only see the
masculine as divine and holy and worthy
of worship while women are presented as
unclean, tempting, feeble-minded, unable
to care for themselves, beneath men and
subject to their self-imposed authority.

## Pussy Worship Throughout the Ages

The power of the pussy is not new. Since the Paleolithic age (read: millions of years ago), civilizations all over the world worshipped the vagina. There are carved figures of women with large breasts and large hips (often called Venus figurines, though they pre-date the Roman goddess Venus) found across civilizations. Festivals and ceremonies were dedicated to the magic and mysteries of the pussy as symbols of fertility. Paintings of pussies can be found on cave walls and allusions to the pussy are ubiquitous throughout ancient and classical art. The pussy was sacred because it brought forth life. Pussy sustained the world as it is the only way to create and produce humans. Pussy represented creative power, a physical portal to the spiritual world.

Africa, the motherland of all people, is where many of the first examples of goddess worship were first discovered. All African traditional religions feature a female creator god and/or female deities that are essential to the function and flow of the Universe and represent some of the most powerful natural forces in the world, like the ocean and the wind. There are far too many African traditional religions and their respective female deities to name here, but there are very many stories from these traditions that illustrate how female deities demanded respect from male deities and humanity at large and were known to use their feminine power to do what needed to be done.

As people migrated out of Africa, they took goddess worship with them and adapted new stories on how the Divine Feminine moved through the world. The goddess Ishtar was revered in Mesopotamia around 3500 B.C. Cakes made for cultural celebrations were molded in triangular forms to represent Ishtar's vagina. Yes, the ancient Mesopotamians were figuratively (and probably literally) eating pussy. Across Europe, cave paintings and carvings — called "Sheela Na Gigs" — of female figures squatting with their exaggerated vulvas spread open were common. Egyptian and Japanese women, inspired by regional goddess lore, would lift their skirts and flash their pussies to increase agricultural harvest and dispel evil and negative energy. The Hawaiian goddess

Kapo is said to have distracted a persistent half-human-half-pig trying to assault her (or her sister Pele, depending on the version of the story) by detaching her vagina and throwing it at him (he subsequently chased her vagina to the end of the earth). Hinduism regards the energy from which all people are created as female, which is represented by the goddess Shakti. The original Kama Sutra, the most notable ancient text on sacred sexuality, refers to the vagina as the "yoni," meaning "sacred space" and symbol of the divine feminine mysteries.

Medieval myths tell a story of how Satan was stunned and defeated when a woman flashed him her vagina. This is part of what began the demonization and fear of the pussy. If pussy could confound Satan himself, it must be evil! Eventually, the patriarchy, high on the thrill of colonization and violence, couldn't bear to see women wield all this power and get all this praise for just being who they are while they would only be praised for their conquests. In the simple man's mind, women didn't deserve all this praise because they hadn't done anything special. Soon began the narrative that men were the creators of the Universe and that people with pussies were weaker, less capable, erratic, and unpredictable; therefore, they could never possibly have such power and all people who believed such were ignorant and needed to be saved (read: needed to start worshipping men) with Christianity.

This Christianity was the version where any mention of the Divine Feminine was removed. You know that

Pussy Prayers

"Jesus fish" you see on bumper stickers? That symbol was originally the pagan *ichthys* associated with the Greek fish-goddess, Atargatis, and was so revered in the Roman Empire that Christian authorities made sure they included it in their misogynist version of Christianity in order to get people interested and deny any previous feminine meaning. They also removed all mention of goddess Asherah who was worshipped by the early Israelites and considered "Queen of Heaven" and "Yahweh's wife." This was the Christianity that painted women like Eve as dangerous, irresponsible, gullible, insubordinate and in need of male leadership (interestingly, snakes have historically been associated with goddesses, so now the snake is demonic and the woman is impure – this is just

ONE Bible story!). Throughout the Middle Ages, thousands of women were burned as witches by Christian leaders because of their "insatiable carnal lust" and the fear of (disguised as disdain for) female sexuality. Painting women as evil and preserving male authority through the erasure of the Divine Feminine was the priority of the ages.

All of this has led us to find fault and shame with our bodies, to make ourselves smaller in order to serve men's egos, and to do everything we can to make our bodies more attractive to men, never learning that simply having a pussy and relishing that power makes us irresistible to anyone blessed to cross our path.

**Treat Yourself Like Holy Ground**

Pussy Prayers

We are created to create, to manifest.
We are the gatekeepers, the alchemists,
divinely designed to turn nonphysical into
the physical. We are holy, sacred spaces in
and of ourselves. That said, think about
the reverence and care you take with holy
places and objects. Think about how
delicately and lovingly you work with
sacred tools and spiritual guides. This
same veneration must be given to
ourselves. The same way you may
supplicate deities with the things that
delight them, so you must also supplicate
yourself with the things that delight you.
Allowing yourself to revel in your
creativity and your desires are what
manifests pleasure. This is the ultimate
power of pussy.

This pleasure and power does not
necessarily have to do with sex. You could

be abstinent, asexual, or celibate and still experience pleasure. Your pleasure consists of how turned on you are by your surroundings, your experiences, and your very being. Yes, your main source of pleasure is *you*. In the next chapters, you will learn exactly how to live in perpetual pleasure to heal and manifest in co-creation with your feminine center.

Some tend to believe that if they have had their uterus removed or damaged in some way then they are now cut off from the center of their divinity, and that is simply not true. Being born woman gives you the innate and untouchable spiritual connection to the Divine, and you can never be disconnected from it. You only need to tap into the frequency, like turning the radio to something you want to listen to in a city where you don't know the local channels. You'll find it eventually and there are plenty of tools to help you along the way.

## You are Here for a Reason

The fact that you have this book implies that you are already releasing the patriarchal restrictions on womanhood that you were most likely raised with. The fact that you have this book is proof that you are searching for truth. When we begin our journey back to ourselves (and we all begin this journey regardless of how we were raised), we tend to look outside of ourselves for answers. We look for books, divinations, communities, online platforms, and anything else that might help us piece together an identity that better resonates with who we know we really are on some level. You may have found yourself at some point seeking to soothe your anxieties and longing for understanding or repressing your mixed emotions through food, sex, drugs, alcohol, and other vices. You may have noticed issues with your reproductive system as you are on this journey of truly understanding your womanhood. You may feel like you are barely holding it together, surviving instead of thriving. You may find yourself constantly comparing yourself and your life to other women and finding fault with them or with yourself. This is common, and it is not permanent. You have taken the first steps. Everything that you seek is within you, and all you need is the right tools to help you excavate all the best parts of yourself. It will take work, and it will take patience, but you will get there, and it will be glorious. Be gentle with yourself, remain open, take responsibility for yourself and your life, and move forward with the intention that you will rediscover all that was missing from your life. You will find acceptance, forgiveness, stability, discernment, safety, confidence, clarity, connection, truth, and freedom.

**Pleasure Principles:**

- This book has been created by and for Black women, femmes, and all Black people who have pussies.

- This book is written in such a way that it is not required that you read it from beginning to end.

- This book is an introduction, not an encyclopedia.

- Patriarchy and toxic masculinity have forced us to dim our light, but this book is the first step in our reclamation and reconnection.

- Be gentle with yourself on this journey.

Pussy Prayers

# CHAPTER TWO

Pussy Prayers

## II
### Attention, Please!

Who taught you about your body? Did they teach you freedom or inhibition? Did they empower your bodily autonomy, or did they demand your chastity? Did they explain to you the connection between the body and the spirit, or were the two concepts completely separate? What did they teach you about pleasure?

## Learning Womanhood

What does it mean to be a woman? Who is a woman and who is not? How did you learn this? Most often, women are biologically and socially defined by the presence and performance of the body parts between their legs, though this is only one part of the feminine experience.

Unless you were born to a tapped-in, turned-on, sexually liberated mother, chances are that your sexuality was one of the first taboos you ever knew. Somebody probably popped your hand if you reached between your legs during diaper changes. Someone probably taught you to "cover up" in front of male family members and friends before you even really knew the difference between male and female bodies. As you got older, you probably realized that the way you felt was not valued. You were taught only to think and do as you were told.

If anyone talked to you about your changing body, your menstrual cycle, or sex, they probably did not go into much detail, if any, about what womanhood is and what it means to be in touch with your feminine power. Instead, if anyone spoke to you at all, it was probably along the lines of warning you against being "fast" and not to bring home any babies. And, unless you were brave, you probably never thought to try to get a good look at the parts between your legs, let alone spend too much time touching down there. No doubt, you probably never knew that pleasure was your birthright.

If your family was religious, then there was an entirely new layer to this repression of feminine power. Patriarchal religious dogma teaches us to remain covered, virginal, and pure. Your body is but a vessel through which you serve God, sacrificing sinful worldly pleasure with the promise of paradise in the afterlife. Women were to remain humble and were most often unclean or somehow defiled but, "by His grace," some man agrees to marry her so that she can fulfill her sole duty of bearing children.

## Historical Trauma

In the Black community, we often find humor and connection in the synchronicities across families and households. It's almost as if we were all raised by the same people. Where did our parents get this stuff from? And, as it pertains to our purpose here, why didn't they better equip us to live healthy spiritual and sexual lives as female-bodied people?

It can be assumed that many of these repressed beliefs stemmed from the enslavement of African people in America. In a time and place where women had their identity and autonomy violently stolen, having no control over where their daughters or they themselves would be taken, forced and ravaged at the will of white plantation owners, our foremothers developed ways to cope, survive, and keep their daughters safe as best they could. We honor and thank them for their love and protection across time and space, as we understand that they were doing their best in this foreign land. However, the direction to cover, diminish, and remove the temptation of your womanliness has led to pervasive shame and disconnection from our bodies to this day. We allow things to happen to us because we are taught to be meek, not to make waves, not to cause trouble, and that our bodies (and essentially our personhood) belong to whatever man is in our life. We tend to ignore that signs and signals that our pussy gives us until it's too late, and some trauma has manifested physically as infertility, fibroids, PCOS, cancer, or some other vaginal or reproductive issue. Only after the fact do we realize how dangerous it is to be disconnected from our pussies.

## The Danger in Disconnection

To be disconnected from our bodies is to be disconnected from our Goddess-given power. To defer the autonomy of our bodies to our fathers or husbands is to defer to the ideas and direction of these men instead of learning to listen to our own internal guidance. In this disassociation, our pussies have gone ignored and our birthright to pleasure gone unknown. But we are waking up. Women everywhere have suddenly noticed the lack and are realizing the need to define ourselves for ourselves. We have gone looking for ourselves, entirely unsure of what we may find. Thank Goddess for the internet! How else would we be able to get back in touch with the innate feminine wisdom we were born with but forced to forget? Facebook groups abound and Amazon carts overflow with pieces and relics of this knowledge that we so desperately seek. This knowledge has never been thoroughly recorded all in one book, and while this book makes an attempt at providing fundamental practices to realign with *who you really are,* the fact remains that this will not be a one-stop shop. In fact, there is only one place that has all the knowledge you seek, and she's sitting with you right now, just below your belly, above your knees, and between your thighs….and she'd like to say hello.

## Self-Taught Sex Ed

My own journey to owning my power through my pussy started at quite a young

age. I was about eight years old when I
decided I wanted to get a good look at my
pussy. I was a latchkey kid, so I had about
three solid hours of alone time at home. I
was (and still am) an avid reader and spent
most of my free time thumbing through
books, writing stories, or watching
television.

I especially loved reading magazines.
One day, I saw my mother's basket of
magazines and wanted to know what was
so different about grown-up magazines
versus the kid/tween magazines that I had
subscriptions to (remember CosmoGirl?).
I plopped down on the living room floor
and grabbed a stack of glossy zines to
review. I don't remember if it was *Ebony*,
or *Essence*, or *Jet*, but I know it was a
magazine with a beautiful Black woman
on the cover. Towards the bottom of the

cover, I saw a word in big, bold, purple
letters: SEX.

I wasn't clear on what sex was at that
point, but I knew it was something I
should not be reading about at my age.
One of my earliest memories is being
reprimanded for saying the word "sex" as
I played pretend in the living room as a
toddler. Naturally, with no threat of
punishment at this moment, I flipped
right over to the page to find out what this
sex thing was all about. Whatever the
article was about went right over my head,
but I never forgot that this was the first
time I saw the word "vagina" in print. I
knew what a vagina was…vaguely. I knew
I had one, and I knew that I had to take
extra care to clean inside it during my
bath. I knew there were some sensitive
parts down there (as I had discovered

during bath time) but touching these parts didn't resonate as pleasure. It was just weird, and I didn't particularly care for it. The grown-ups in this magazine, though, seemed to be really interested in their vaginas.

There was a part of the article that said to take a hand mirror and put it between your legs so that you could see what your vagina looked like. *Looked like?* I never thought there might be anything to look at. I checked the clock. There was still about an hour left before my mom was due home. That was plenty of time to try out this mirror thing. I put all the magazines back in the basket and went searching our little apartment for a hand mirror to no avail. Clever as I was, I went into the bathroom and realized that the large mirror covered the wall and ended where the bathroom counter began. I could stand on the counter and see my entire little body from head to toe. I had the idea that if I sat up on the counter without my pants, faced the mirror, leaned back and spread my legs, I could get a full view of my pussy.

I was astounded. It was like a whole universe in there! I remember thinking it reminded me of the moon, with its hills and holes and crevices. I stared and poked and prodded until I tired of leaning back on the hard counter. "*Wow*," I thought to myself. "*So that's a vagina. Huh. A pretty fancy thing just to pee out of.*" I had no concept of what it was for other than that. I was fully indifferent to that space between my legs. It was what it was, and if it was supposed to do something special, then mine must have been broken. It

would be a few years before I revisited my
pussy again.

I remember my first instance of shame
around my pussy. Not long after I had
discovered my pussy for myself, I was
with my mother at a hotel we were staying
at while we traveled for her job. I came
out of the bathroom after a shower and,
not yet having any qualms about nudity at
all, dropped my towel in front of my
mother and began the process of getting
ready for bed. My mother had been on the
phone with her best friend at the time and
scared me to death when she yelled,
"WHAT THE HELL?!" I turned to look
at her, terrified that maybe I had done
something wrong, or she had seen
something that I needed to get away from,
like a bug or a mouse. Before I could ask
her what was wrong, she announced to

me (and her friend on the phone) "THERE'S HAIR ON YOUR BOO-BOO!" "Boo-boo" was the baby term my mom taught me instead of vagina, but I let her think I didn't know what vagina was. I didn't want to have that conversation. And I wasn't sure I was ready to have this one. *Hair?* Well, yeah. There was hair. I thought nothing of it. I'm a hairy girl. I have hair all over my body, including my chest, feet, fingers, and toes (as an adult, I can see this was probably the onset of the hormonal issues I would encounter just a couple of years later). My mother was freaking out and telling her friend about my pubic hair. She made me lay down on the bed so she could get a better look (and describe it to her friend on the phone). "How long has this been here?" she asked urgently. I honestly didn't know. Seemed

like it just showed up one day. I didn't
think to mark the date. I'm eight years old.
How was I supposed to know that this
was significant? My mother continued
examining my body and relaying the
information to her friend. As I lie there
waiting for it to be over, I felt my face get
hot. I was embarrassed. I felt like I had
done something wrong. I felt like
something was wrong with my body.
After that, I tread carefully around other
girls my age. I felt different. I felt ashamed
of my body. It must have been doing
something that none of the other girls'
bodies did. This was the extent of the
conversation my mother ever had with me
about my body, and thus began the
resentment of my pussy.

My sentiments toward my pussy only
worsened when I got my first period at

age ten, on the first day of middle school. Of all the days in a tween girl's life, why did my first period and my first day of middle school have to coincide? My periods were heavy, lasted more than a week, and came with debilitating cramps and nausea. I felt like my pussy was only there to cause me pain, embarrassment, and inconvenience.

A couple years later, the topic of sex came up again. I was interested as I heard my classmates begin to talk about sexual things they had done with other classmates. I had no way of knowing if these stories were true, but it sounded cool. Around this time was the first time I was propositioned for sex. It wasn't the first time I had received sexual attention, as my booty and breasts made their debut in elementary school. But this was the first time a boy had explicitly stated his desire to have sex with me. *Sex?* Still wasn't clear on the concept. Still wasn't thrilled with my pussy. I ignored both the proposition and my pussy for a while longer until one day I saw a new bold word on the front of one of my mother's magazines – ORGASM.

*What...what is that? What does that even mean?* As luck would have it, I still had plenty of alone time after school and the magazine article provided step by step instructions on how to have an orgasm by yourself in various ways. Though still out of touch with my pussy, it sounded like a fun thing to try while I had the time and the privacy. I decided to try the method that required me to get into the bathtub, lay on my back, and let the water from the faucet crash down over the area I learned was called a clitoris (this was also my first experience clearing the browsing history on the house computer. I had to Google a lot of strange things to figure this one out).

So, I do it. I'm lying there, water running, trying to figure out how I was going to explain my wet hair to my mother when such an overwhelming feeling of pleasure bubbled up inside me that I thought I was going to explode. Wave after wave of water and incredible energy crashed over my body until I realized I was curled up in the fetal position, half submerged in the tub, and I was out of breath. *What just happened?! What did my body just do? Was that normal?* I had no way of knowing. I assumed that I had experienced my first orgasm. From that day on, I knew I needed way more of that. And often. Still, I had no real connection with my pussy. I knew now what it could do, but I wasn't particularly interested in it otherwise.

The same year I learned to orgasm would end up being the same year I began to experience sexual abuse at the hands of male family members. The year after that would be when I had sex for the first time and the year that my period stopped. It had been perfectly regular, month after month, and then…nothing.

In a panic, I told my mother that I hadn't gotten my period. I feared the worst – pregnancy. My mother had no reason to assume this was the reason for my disappearing period, so she scheduled a doctor's appointment for me. "You haven't been having sex, have you?" asked the doctor in front of my mother. My mother had refused to leave the room during this line of questioning, even at the doctor's request. I told her I hadn't as I felt my mother's eyes burning a hole in the side of my face.

The doctor, a tall and broad Black woman, announced that she would be conducting a pregnancy test just in case, but that the most likely cause for my period stopping was PCOS – Polycystic Ovarian Syndrome. She didn't give me too many details about it except that it could only be proven through a checklist of symptoms (one of which is extra hair growth – surprise, surprise) or an ultrasound. After checking off almost every symptom on the list, the doctor simply said, "Well, you will probably just have an irregular period, and you can take birth control pills to regulate it. You might have trouble having children later on, but birth control can regulate that, too." And with that, the doctor excused herself from the room.

I wasn't pregnant. That was good to know. But here I was with a dysfunctional pussy, yet another reason to resent this awful mess between my legs. At that point, I remember thinking that all my pussy was good for was getting attention, having sex, and having orgasms. It was an object for pleasure outside of myself, not connected to me, but there anyway. I carried this notion throughout my teen years as I used my pussy as an object for sex.

It wasn't enjoyable. Sex was painful for me, physically and emotionally. My willingness to fulfill the desires of my male classmates and some men much older made me feel worthy and functional outside of myself in a way that I did not feel inside. I still carried the shame that something was wrong with my body, with my pussy; that other girls were normal and I wasn't. That shame, coupled with the anxiety and depression that comes with PCOS, made me disconnect from my body even more. On top of that, realizing in my early teen years that I was attracted to girls more than boys, I felt even more dysfunctional. I didn't want to be seen. I didn't want to be touched. I wanted to be comforted, to be loved, and to be told that I was okay, that I was normal.

In an effort to make myself feel better, feel full of something, and to forget all of my anxieties, I began to binge eat in secret, skip school to smoke weed with my friends, and barely slept. Through high school, I watched myself balloon into a person I didn't recognize. None of my clothes fit anymore. My mother, kind as she is, attributed my ill-fitting fashions to the "cheap manufacturers" or "the dryer shrinking all the clothes." I guess she didn't want to admit that her little girl was quite a big girl. Looking back at my prom pictures, it is surprising that no one said anything to me about my rapid weight gain. Then again, I did grow up in the South, and since there were plenty of girls larger than I was, I was often considered "thick" and therefore still attractive. No one realized I was trying to hide from them, that I still felt broken, that I dealt with anxiety and depression, that having PCOS meant my body was extremely sensitive to unhealthy foods, that I had been a victim of abuse, and that I was only existing in my head, never in my body.

It was not long after this that I found myself on the path that would lead me back to my divinity. I had no idea at the time, but I would spend the next decade falling into an intimate communion with the Universe, getting to the root causes of my physical and emotional states, and realizing just how out of touch with my body I had become. I had to do the work of unpacking all of the reasons why I had secluded myself into my head and covered myself with this protective layer. I had to come to the understanding of where my womanly power truly came from, and that, in order to embrace that power, I had to reconnect with the epicenter of my being.

## You Are Not Alone

I described the first part of my story here so that you might see some of yourself in it. I want you to know that you are not alone in the things you did not know or the habits you may have had before you learned better. If part of my past is your current reality, I hope that you do not feel exposed but, rather, in good company.

The state of our pussy is usually a reflection of our mental and emotional conditions and our physical actions. When we are living well, honoring and respecting ourselves, speaking truth to our experiences, and healing as necessary, we can be vessels of creativity, beauty, strength, and power. When we ignore the pussy and all of her experiences, traumas, and cries for attention, we can often link that to the onset of illnesses both physical and mental.

All we can do is start from where we are. Do not be afraid to acknowledge your ignorance. You made decisions or mistakes based on what you understood at the time. Be gentle with unpacking your pain so that you can grow. At a certain point, our pussies have a way of leading us to exactly where we need to be in order to find our healing in divine timing. The fact that you are here means that your pussy is calling for your attention. Let her lead you to your reconciliation, to the reclamation of your pleasure.

## Pleasure Principles:

- The way that we have been taught about ourselves, our bodies, and our sexuality stem from historical trauma.
- We all need a do-over in comprehensive sexuality education – you are not alone.
- Start where you are and be patient with yourself.
- The state of our pussy is usually a reflection of our mental and emotional conditions and our physical actions.
- Your pussy will lead you to exactly what you need, exactly when you need it.

# Reclamation

## CHAPTER THREE

# III
## Reclamation

You deserve a happy pussy. It is your right and your responsibility. This starts with the reconnection to your feminine power, which requires the explicit recommitment and reclamation of your body. Begin with the understanding and remembrance of the fact that you are divine. You are the direct offspring of God and Goddess, a literal embodiment of the universe. This section of the book is meant to help you get back into your body, connect with your pussy, and prepare for a new life of #EverydayDeliciousness.

## Tend to Your Temple

Think of your body as a temple. Is it in pristine condition — fit for a goddess — or is the paint chipping and the windows broken? Is there seating open and available for dedicated worshippers, or are they occupied by all the things people have left behind? Have you allowed thieves into your temple? What have they taken that needs to be restored? Is the temple garden blossoming, or has it been forgotten and left to its own devices

— overgrown, under-watered, stretched beyond its limits, and in need of rest?

However you have or haven't been tending to your temple, this section of the book is going to help you clear everything out and start again so that you can begin to cultivate seeds of self-love and daily pleasure. Before we bring in the new, we have to deal with the old. All that stuff that you haven't confronted or tried to bury needs to come up and out.

## My Clearing Process

My clearing process began when I was twenty years old. I had been invited to a sister circle that was started by an older friend of mine. A group of about ten women congregated weekly over the course of a summer to discuss our experiences of womanhood. One weekend, my friend had contacted a healer who specialized in womb saunas (also known as vaginal steaming). All this new age woo-woo stuff was foreign to me at this point, but it sounded intriguing and I was on board for any time I got to spend with my sister circle. Before beginning the process, I answered a few survey questions about my background, health, and sexual experiences. The healer met us at my friend's home on the day of and conducted the womb saunas in my friend's bedroom. Depending on our individual experiences and needs, a blend of herbs was crafted and placed in boiling water. The basin of hot water and herbs was placed underneath a chair with a hole in the seat. We were instructed to get completely naked and sit on the seat.

Then, we were wrapped in a thick cape to keep the steam in while also keeping us warm and covered. Next, the healer gave us crystals to hold in each hand, depending on the attributes she felt we needed.

This healer was also psychic, and, as we sat through our steaming, we discussed various life events that affected our relationships with our pussies. It was here that I first spoke of my sexual abuse out loud and to another person. I was able to process the complicated emotions I had around being violated and my response to my trauma by engaging sexually with anyone who would have me. Through this process, the healer stated that the natural state of my pussy (she used the term "womb") was one of joy. She also told me that my experiences would prepare me to be someone who worked on behalf of women and sexuality. The exact term she used was "sex goddess," which was absurd to me at the time. She gave us individual homework following our steam. My assignment was to write down every single sexual encounter that I had ever had, as far back as I could remember. By identifying these experiences, I could begin to process and release them.

This was not a quick and dirty process. It took me months of listing names I could remember, leaving the list alone for a while, coming back to it when another name and experience came to mind. The more I allowed these experiences to be remembered, the more they seemed to come. Once I felt like I had finally finished the list, it was longer than I thought it should be for only

75

twenty years of life. I spent some time sitting with the emotions that came up from listing and reviewing every sexual experience I had ever had up to that point. Mostly, I felt anger and shame: anger at being violated, shame for willingly sharing my body with so many who did not treasure it the way it deserved to be treasured.

It was almost as if my pussy knew that I was trying to heal my relationship with her. Like magic, I was suddenly led to books and people that would play major parts in helping me to understand the way my traumas manifested in my body and in my life. From there, I was able to do the work it took to heal it once and for all. I realized that I was diagnosed with PCOS and began rapidly gaining weight around the same time that I began repressing my abuse and having indiscriminate sex. I also realized that, up to that point, I had never been given an orgasm from these sexual encounters, no matter how hard I tried to concentrate and make it happen. I knew that I had to process and heal emotionally and spiritually before I could heal physically. Again, the process was not a quick one. Instead, it took numerous years, repeating of mistakes, and greatly humbling moments for me to fully understand how to embrace my truest self and my natural power.

## First Steps

There are a number of ways for you to begin your own clearing process and begin healing on every level. The first

step is to determine how to connect with
your pussy. Here's a ritual that you can try:

*Find a quiet, safe place where you will be
uninterrupted for a while. Make sure this space is
comfortable for you to sit or lie down. You can
change the atmosphere if you'd like by lighting
candles, burning incense, surrounding yourself
with crystals, or anything else that feels
appropriate.*

*Close your eyes and direct your energy and
attention towards your pelvic area while you place
your hands palms-down on your vulva. Breathe
deeply and make sure your body is relaxed.*

*Begin to speak to your pussy, either out loud
or in your mind. Say whatever feels natural to
you. State your intention to reconnect with her and
heal your body so that you can embrace your*

*natural power and experience pleasure at every level.*

*After you state your intention, remain in the same position and just listen. Pay attention to what comes to mind, especially if these thoughts do not seem to be your own. This is your center, your connection to the Universe, your pussy, communicating with you.*

*Feel free to continue this conversation or to record what comes to you. Continue this process of communicating with your pussy on a regular basis. You can ask her questions, apologize to her, express gratitude for her, or anything else that comes to you. If she does not seem to speak immediately, that's okay. Keep trying. You are rebuilding your relationship with her.*

Pussy Prayers

*Notice any physical sensations that may happen in your pelvic area. You may feel pain or discomfort while you do this work. This is your pussy's way of processing any energy that may be lying stagnant there. As you continue this work over days, weeks, or even months, you should begin to feel more pleasant, turned-on, and empowered in your "prayers" with your pussy. The more pleasure you feel, the more you can be sure that your connection with your pussy is becoming stronger.*

Other methods of energetic clearing can involve the use of various tools and ingredients. Yoni eggs are one such tool that can aid in processing the energy in and around your pussy. These are egg-shaped crystals that can remove stagnant energy or infuse the characteristics of the crystal. Yoni eggs are inserted into the vagina and left there at your discretion or until it decides to come down on its own. Eggs that are good for clearing and cleansing are stones like obsidian and rose quartz (more ideas for crystals to use in a later chapter). Do your research on which stones can be used internally and which stones should only be used externally, or else you can risk giving yourself infections or poisoning yourself with unsafe materials.

Another method of cleansing is vaginal steaming. This is typically done by sitting over a pot or bowl of hot water with herbs (like tea) and letting the steam enter your vagina to infuse the healing properties into your pussy. There are resources in Part Two of this book to help you cultivate your practice for healing and pleasure.

A major part of the clearing process is a detoxification of all that you consume. This includes everything that you watch, listen to, speak, eat, drink, and allow to enter your immediate space as well as your body. There are no crystals, steams, or meditations that are going to be effective if you have not prioritized your physical health. Step-by-step instructions for detoxing your physical body and environment are listed in Part Two.

## Consistency and Intention

The most important part of all of these rituals is consistency and intention. This is not a one-and-done type of deal. Develop a schedule for this work. Most people find that daily and weekly activities are most convenient and beneficial. Do not use your schedule or other obligations as an excuse. Use the free time that you have wisely and do things that work for you. Who told you that you "had time"? Why is your wellness not an urgent priority? The more excuses you make, the more time you spend disconnected from all the things you claim you want. Make a decision, choose yourself, and make it work for you, your schedule, and your life. If you have time for television and the internet, you have time for yourself. Make the commitment to yourself, to your pussy, and you will find that everything you desire falls into place. This will be the most loving and loyal relationship you will ever choose to enter.

Maintain the sincere intention of cleansing and clearing on every level of your being and reconnecting with your pussy. And pay close attention to her. Pay attention when something (sexual or non-sexual) turns you on or when it turns you completely off. Pay attention to anything that makes you feel anxious or afraid. Pay attention to when you feel well and when you don't. Pay attention to any symptoms that your pussy might be showing you — burning, itching, odor, etc.

Pay attention to the messages you receive, seemingly out of nowhere. The ideas, the questions, the answers, the actions you feel led to take — all of these are the ways that your pussy is trying to communicate with you and let you know what it needs. Make note of these divine downloads. Write them down in a place that you can get to quickly and refer to often. When she speaks, don't be afraid to speak back. Have conversations. Talk to

your body. Encourage yourself. Question
yourself. Laugh, play, sing, dance, and
learn to just BE with yourself. This is the
start of you stepping into your power,
taking control of your pleasure, staying
away from anything that does not serve
you, and manifesting your truest desires.

## Your Pussy Wants What's Best For You

Your pussy, your physical center of
sacred feminine intuition and power,
wants what's best for you and wants your
full attention and commitment as you
embark on this journey. Your pussy
desperately wants to reconnect with you
and will manifest whatever situations and
emotions it needs to in order for that to
happen. I caution all those who are
comfortable with their current situation

and dislike change not to go through with this process. However, the fact that you are reading this makes me think that you are willing to make changes necessary to step into your divine pussy power.

As you progress through this work, you may notice the loss of or extreme displeasure for certain people, places, and things. This is your pussy's way of letting you know that these are not things that she likes. These are not things that are increasing your pleasure. To embark on this work means to strip away all that does not serve you for your highest good.

## Beware of the Ego

In this work, you will encounter your ego trying to keep you in the same place you've always been. Your ego sounds like a hater. Your ego is speaking when your thoughts are not encouraging your healing, but instead telling you all the reasons why it won't work, why you should stop, or why all this effort is a waste of time. The ego gets a bad rap for the way that it manifests, but it's actually trying to keep you safe. Safety to your ego means, "I did this before and I didn't die so this is safe." Therefore, anything new and risky registers as a threat and must be discouraged. Fears, frustrations, and "fuck this" moments will happen. Your job is to talk yourself out of spiraling. Allow your higher self to soothe your ego. Thank your ego for its concern for your safety and assure it that you're okay, and everything you are doing is for your highest good. This will take practice, but once you master it, you will be unstoppable.

## Own Your Truth

Part of reclamation and reconnection is revealing the story that underlies the disconnect with your pussy. Understanding this story helps you to pinpoint exactly where certain habits started and give you a reference point for how to change that story. This does not have to be long, and it might help to imagine telling the story from the perspective of your pussy. Using my own story as an example, I might write down the following:

*The attention that people gave me (the pussy)
caused us to feel embarrassed and ashamed.
Manifestations of trauma in our physical body
have caused her (the person) to see me as an
inconvenience and as broken. She has tried her
best to avoid me unless she believes that allowing
others access to me will bring the love and
acceptance she has not yet learned to give herself.*

Unpacking this story is the start of understanding exactly where the disconnect happened. Explore your relationship with your pussy and take as long as you need to fully understand all that has happened. It's okay if you do not know where to start in healing these things. Unpacking them will happen over time with consistent effort and intention. Trust that your pussy wants to work with you to reconnect and heal. Trust that she

89

wants the best for you and intuition and guidance that compels you is her way of guiding you on the right path.

## What Does Your Inner Child Need?

Another way to begin rewriting your story is to imagine you are your younger self again. Whichever age comes to you, imagine that you can tell your young self exactly what she needed to hear at that time. Write to her, sing to her, imagine hugging her, holding her, comforting her, whatever she needs.

You may find that this reimagining may heal old, repressed emotional wounds that you have been carrying in your womb space for years. Express any emotions that come up for you any way you see fit. Cry, scream, write, or anything else that feels good in that moment. Intend to empty yourself so that you can begin to refill yourself with what you deserve. If you'd like to write down your negative emotions and then burn them as a representation of release and renewal, do that. Do not shame or criticize yourself for your emotions. Do not try to numb yourself or project your feelings onto people closest to you. Do not try to rationalize or logic your way out of feeling. Feel everything in your body deeply and fully. You are healing, and all is well.

The point of all of this is to express your truth. You must express every feeling fully, no matter how painful or inconvenient, no matter how much it negates stereotypes of who you should be or how you should behave. Holding your truth back is what has gotten you to this place, so you must do something different to move past it and move back towards the woman you were created to be. As you move through this work, check back in with the Pressure Points from chapter one. Has anything changed? Why do you think that is?

_____

**Pleasure Principles:**

- You deserve a happy pussy. It is your right and your responsibility.
- Your body is a temple. Reflect on how you've been caring for it.
- There are processes through which you can begin to physically and energetically work through, clear, and cleanse negativity and obstacles blocking your pleasure.
- There are no shortcuts around healing your hurts.
- Seeking professional help is encouraged for processing traumatic events.

Pussy Prayers

# Everyday Deliciousness

## CHAPTER FOUR

# IV
## Everyday Deliciousness

Once you have done the work of clearing out the negativity, stagnation, trauma, and other energies in your pussy that have not allowed you to hear her voice and walk in pleasure, you must engage in the work of filling yourself up with the pleasure you deserve. Remember, the more pleasure you experience, the more power you have. You are a place on

Earth for the divine to reside, a walking, talking, living, breathing temple. The same way a church must be kept and maintained is the same way you must care for yourself. Self-care is a divine responsibility and the key to living a juicy, delicious life. Do not allow worldly obligations and patriarchal influences to make you neglect yourself. Make the commitment to yourself to regularly engage in your pleasure. Treat yourself like the goddess you are. Remind yourself that you deserve positive attention, and you deserve for time to be made for you.

## It Ain't Always Love and Light

Please note that engaging in this work and pursuing your pleasure does not mean that you have to be happy, shiny, love,

and light at all times. If that is not truly
how you feel, then that is not pleasure.
Pleasure lies in going with the flow of
your emotions. If you are angry, it might
feel really good to scream or throw
something (safely, of course). That is still
pleasure. If you are sad, listening to
emotional music in the dark by yourself
can make you feel understood and
acknowledged. This is still pleasure.
Honor how you truly feel.

Trust that your pussy is guiding you to
ultimate pleasure, even if it may seem like
you are experiencing grief, loss, or pain. In
order for you to have everything you
desire and everything that is intended for
your highest good, you must be okay with
releasing that which does not serve you,
things you are clinging to but are not good
for you, and things that you do not really

want but have held on to anyway. Allow yourself to move through your emotions. Grieve and feel deeply, as this is our divine right and natural ability. This is not an exercise in perfection. We contain multitudes and we deserve to embody all aspects of ourselves. You are on the path to becoming the woman you were created to be.

This work cannot simply be read and understood. This work must be felt at every level, allowing you to gauge the resonance and connection you have as your markers of progress. Pay attention to the sensations your body is giving you, as these are indicators of messages you need to "hear." She will whisper, so you must listen closely. Ignoring these messages will put you at risk for the physical and emotional manifestations of repression and negativity. Identify when you tend to be most emotional (hint: it's probably right before or during your menstrual cycle). This is the time to tune in to the messages being sent your way: acknowledge them, express your emotions, and make any necessary changes lest you bubble up and emotionally burst all over the nearest bystander.

## Your Menstrual Cycle

This is your most powerful and sensitive time as a woman. If you do not have a typical period, pay attention to how you feel around the full and new moons. During the times when you feel hyper-aware of everything, emotional, wanting to be alone to reflect, this is your spiritual "moon time." Our natural processes do not end because we are without certain body parts or physical experiences. We are beings made of mostly water, and just as the ocean tide is affected by the lunar phases, so are we. Do not focus so much on having a period that comes on the full or new moon if it doesn't already happen that way. As you become more aware of and in tune with your spiritual and sexual nature, whilst working through healing on every level, you will find that you will naturally begin to have your "moon time" at the perfect time for you.

Honor your feelings and desires during this time. In doing so, you can download all kinds of information about you, your life, where to revise and how to move forward. Acknowledging these messages is key. If the urge to explore divinatory tools such as astrology, tarot, pendulum, or others arises, this is a good time to explore these things as your intuition is heightened during this time. You will be able to read people and energies more easily, so if you feel like you don't want to deal with certain people, go with that inclination. Pay attention to your dreams, as they may be more frequent, lucid, or prophetic. Journaling can help keep track of thoughts and feelings during this time. Review these journal entries outside of the window of your period to see if any divine downloads make more sense for your life at that time.

Remember that your period (however it looks for you) is a physical sign of your fertility (literal or metaphorical). Notice if your period changes when you are being a creative force, actively moving towards your desires, bringing forth life to your ideas and projects, or when you are suppressing your creative impulses, not moving towards pleasure, or remaining in situations that are less than ideal. Also notice if you feel disconnected from your body and your intuition if you use a birth control that shortens or suppresses your period.

If your period is marked by pain, mood changes, and other symptoms assigned to Pre- or Post-Menstrual Syndrome (PMS), this is your body's way of trying to get your attention. Take the time to slow down and listen to your body. If it is telling you to do something or stop something, listen, and do what you need to do. If you need to rest, then prioritize that. If you have the overwhelming urge to address something you've been trying to ignore, address it. If you begin to feel like something in your body is not as it should be, go to the doctor. If you realize that you've been holding on to something that is not serving you, let it go. Ignoring your intuition during this time will only cause more issues to manifest physically and emotionally.

Many women are raised to hate their periods. We are taught shame, disgust, denial, and suppression of our periods. Men have called us "unclean," and have used our periods as excuses to dismiss our feelings, which results in us grappling with embarrassment and resentment. We have been conditioned to believe our periods are inconvenient and should be ignored as much as possible. These beliefs have kept us disconnected from our pussies and

from our power. If you have a negative
relationship with your menstrual cycle,
begin by reclaiming this time as a period
(no pun intended) of immense closeness
between you and the Divine. Reflect on
how you learned to relate to your
menstrual cycle and write down that story
so that you can begin to heal and change
it.

**Get Into The Flow**

The more you acknowledge the
messages your pussy has for you, the less
you need outside forces to come and
teach you hard lessons. The more
confident you are in your connection with
your pussy, the more you are able to
maintain boundaries and take
responsibility for yourself, and the less

you care what people think of you. The more you give attention to this sacred center of yourself, the easier it is to identify your passion and your purpose. Life does not have to be difficult and full of coping, climbing, striving, busyness, and fear. Tapping into your pussy power means tapping into the flow. In flow, things you need come easily, ideas flourish, passions are exciting, and purpose is easy to move into.

It helps to "go with the flow" of your natural energy as much as possible. For example, during your "moon time," do as much as you can to rest and restore yourself. The week after this, you may find yourself inspired and ready to create and renew yourself or a life situation. The following week, typically the week of ovulation, you may feel more sensual, having the desire for intimacy, connection, and expression. After this comes a week of slowing down, listening to yourself, and addressing your needs. It would feel unnatural and depleting to create and express when your pussy is telling you to slow down and rest. Honor these natural waves of energy and find your pleasure in each of them.

## Pleasure Rituals

The next part of this chapter will outline a number of rituals that you can adopt to aid in your self-care practice, increase your pleasure and, as a result, increase your power. These practices are not in any particular order, and you can choose any combination of these that feel good to you. Remember: if it doesn't feel good, don't do it. You can use your comfort level with each exercise to measure how much you are healing your relationship with your pussy and able to reconnect with your source of pleasure. But, if something just doesn't do it for you, that's okay, too.

These are not one-and-done rituals. They are also not rigid in that they have to be followed exactly as written. They are intentionally brief so that you may personalize them and change them to suit you. By no means is this list exhaustive. You should create your own pleasure rituals that are meaningful to you. Consistency and intention are key. There are additional resources and exercises in Part Two of this book.

## Morning Ritual

Establish a morning practice that you can move into naturally after waking. This practice should not be something that you dread but something to look forward to and starts your day in such a way that you move through the world fully in tune with your Goddess-self. The more in tune with pleasure you are, the more every other aspect of your life will be pleasurable. Check in with your body and determine how each part of your body feels. Are you in any pain or discomfort? Place one hand on any part of the body that does not feel well and rest the other on top of your pussy. Feel the discomfort and ask your pussy what the reason behind it might be.

What is the discomfort trying to tell you and what do you need to do to heal so that you can return to your natural state of pleasure? Listen to and record whatever comes up. Follow this by speaking healing and wellness over your body while you lay hands on the parts of yourself that need it.

Creating sacred space should also be part of your morning ritual. Clean, listen to music, burn incenses, light candles, use singing bowls, hold crystals, or anything else that is pleasurable and stimulating to your senses and your energy. You should be feeling at ease, maybe even giddy or aroused, by this sensual practice. This is going to set the tone for the day. Make it meaningful to you.

Engage in some form of movement to get the energy flowing through your body. If working out in the gym or doing aerobic exercises feels good to you, then do that. If not, don't do it. Choose dance or yoga or jumping on a trampoline — anything that is going to be pleasurable to you.

You could also begin your day with affirmations. Speak over yourself with intentions for your life, your day, your work, or anything else you might encounter on this day. Acknowledge the blessings that have manifested in your life and meditate in gratitude for them. Acknowledge the seemingly negative events in your life and be grateful for those as well, as everything is for your highest good.

**Learn What You Love**

Learn what you love and leave what you don't. Throughout your life, get rid of anything that's been annoying or stressful to you. In all of your choices, determine what will bring you the most pleasure and go wholeheartedly after that. What you believe will bring you pleasure may change and adjust along the way and that's okay. The point is to practice allowing yourself to be led by your pussy and bring the most pleasure into your life. Do not compromise on your pleasure! Your pussy remembers who you are and who've you been across reincarnations. Your pussy may delight in opulence, outrageousness, and extravagance. She may enjoy minimalism, calm, and quiet. Go with

whatever feels best. Remember, your
pleasure is your power.

## Get Your Glamour On

Feeling sensual and beautiful is one of
the most pleasurable parts of being a
woman. The way that you show up in the
world can literally change the energy,
attitudes, and experience of the spaces you
enter. Think about how much power you
command over a room when people
notice your beauty, smell the fragrance
you're wearing, hear the sweetness and
timbre of your voice. Invoke the senses
and remind people that a goddess is in the
room!

There are a number of ways to
manifest more beauty and pleasure in
yourself. Take special care in your bathing

113

rituals, using only the most enticing scents and nontoxic, effective products. As you bathe and moisturize your body, speak over your products and over your body with your intentions for radiance, beauty, and pleasure. Remember, these practices should delight and excite you.

When getting dressed, wear the clothes that make you feel your best. Adorn your body with accessories like body chains and waist beads that remind you of your sensuality. Wear makeup if it excites you to enhance your natural beauty this way. Any way that you choose to present yourself to the world is for your pleasure.

Do not forget to cleanse and adorn your pussy along with the rest of your body. If you feel the need to use products, use mild, natural cleansers specifically formulated for your pussy. Use your hands instead of your washcloth to work the cleanser in and around your vulva and outer vaginal area, the places where sweat, lint, and other things can accumulate. Rinse well, then moisturize your pussy with natural oils (like coconut or a blend specifically formulated for your pussy). Stay away from unnatural scents and toxic products for your pussy. Pussy should smell like pussy, your own unique scent, not like fruits or fragrance. If you notice particularly foul smells (anything that reminds you of fish, garbage, or musty armpits), be diligent about your (gentle!) cleansing practice and see a doctor if it persists. Do not insert any cleansers inside the "hole" also known as your vagina. The vagina itself is self-cleaning and needs no help from products.

Pussy Prayers

If you remove hair from your pussy,
you must be diligent about caring for the
skin there. You can treat your pussy to
"facials" the same way you would with
your face in order to soothe and tone the
skin on the vulva and avoid blemishes or
irritation. The best products to use are
plant-based or from the earth (like clay),
made with herbs and ingredients you
recognize. Wear cotton panties if you
choose (at the very least, make sure the
panties you wear have cotton in the area
that touches your vaginal opening). You
want to let your pussy breathe as much as
possible, so don't wear those panties to
bed if you don't have to.

Beauty in, beauty out. If you want to
maintain your external beauty, your
internal self needs attention as well. Drink
plenty of water, teas, and natural juices to

keep your skin and organs hydrated. Eat juicy fruits and vegetables at each meal for all your necessary nutrients. Make sure you are going to the bathroom as much as you are eating and drinking. Waste trapped inside your body can manifest as odor, illness, and blemishes on the skin.

## Sex Magic and Manifesting

Your sexual energy is some of the most powerful energy in the universe. This is the energy that creates worlds. You can use this energy to attract and manifest everything that you desire. Tapping into this sexual energy at any point in the day or in any situation will give you that much more confidence and power. You can be aroused by yourself at any given moment. If you want to attract and influence certain people, dip into your pussy and dab some of your juicy essence behind your ears or on the places where you would typically put perfume. People will be enamored with you everywhere you go.

If you like to feel like you have a little secret that no one knows, go without panties or in your fanciest lingerie under your clothes for no other reason than your own pleasure. During sex or masturbation, before or after orgasm (or during orgasm, if you can focus!), visualize what you want to manifest and let the sexual energy you have building up bring forth your desires. You could try masturbating while repeating your intention over and over until you reach your highest state of pleasure. If you really want to challenge yourself, when you are at your peak state of turn-on, use that arousal to create something physical. Work on a project you've been thinking of, paint, write, sing – do whatever has been yearning to be birthed from you. Surround yourself (safely) with male energy or male-dominated spaces every now and then to remind yourself of what your sexuality and feminine energy feels like and see what arises in you.

Consider how often you sit with your thighs locked together or crossed because you learned in childhood that "ladies sit with their legs closed." If your pussy is your manifestation portal and you consistently keep her constricted and closed off, what do you think that does to your ability to manifest? Practice keeping your legs uncrossed (maintaining modesty as much as you desire) and affirming to your pussy that you are open to allowing your manifestations to be birthed through you.

In all of these rituals, remember that whatever you think about will manifest in your body and in your physical experience, so think carefully and immediately turn away from negative or defeating thoughts. Tell a new story.

## Rewrite Your Story

Because you have identified your old story, full of trauma and negativity, you can clear that out and prepare a new story for yourself. Allow yourself to be rebirthed through this story. Write your new story to include what you would love to be true about you. Read this to yourself each day and whenever you feel yourself moving back towards your old negative story. Visualize your highest self, the self you want to present to the world. Manifest this story into being. If you can conceive it, it is already true.

**Powerful Connections**

Make a daily habit of engaging and activating your breasts, butt, hips, thighs, and all the other sensitive parts of you. You may massage them or stimulate them as you see fit. Pinch your own nipples. Slap your own ass. Dance barefoot in the rain or let the sun shine on parts of you that are usually always covered. Get used to feeling your body in a state of arousal and turn-on, as this is your natural state of being. The power that comes from your pleasure is the power that manifests your desires.

## Send Yourself Nudes

You don't actually have to send nude pictures to yourself or anyone else (unless that's what you're into), but you should definitely take them. With as much discretion and modesty as you desire, practice taking sexy photos of yourself in clothes that make you feel sexy, fun lingerie, or butt-ass naked if you choose. Admire your body, your unique features, and see how much you can arouse yourself with your own private peep show. If it feels uncomfortable or unflattering to do this, sit with those feelings and try to find the root of them. The point of this is to pursue pleasure and feel good. If it's not feeling good, move on from this and come back at a later time.

## Pussy Decisions

When you have to decide something or are wondering what you should do to remain in your power and on the path to pleasure, ask your pussy. Greet her, praise her, lay your hands on her, and simply ask what it is you're thinking about. Listen to her and remember what comes up. Follow her lead. It could be as simple as what you should eat or what you should wear, or as complex as if you should stay in your current home, choose a certain job, or keep a certain partner. Allow your pussy to remind you to be bold. Let pleasure guide you.

## Cleaning Your Castle

Make sure that your living space is pleasant to you. Anything that is unpleasant to you, remove it or change it as much as possible. It should bring you pleasure and comfort to step into your space, not anxiety or shame. Organize, decorate, clean, and arrange in the ways that feel good to you. Clean out your closets and drawers and only leave the clothes and shoes that make you feel best, even your underwear and your lounge-around-the-house clothes. Open cabinets and drawers and make sure they are organized in a way that makes it easy and pleasant to get what you need. This is your external sacred space and should be cared for as such.

## Brag On Your Pussy

Celebrate the marvelous things you've been able to manifest, the things you have in your life that you love, and the things that go well and easily for you. Give gratitude for these things and the things that may not have been positive but have ultimately worked out in your favor. We are often taught that we must be humble, shy, and meek. We are told that we shouldn't brag or else people will say we "think too much of ourselves," or people will be uncomfortable and offended with our reminder of their lack. Why shouldn't we think very much of ourselves?

Talk about what you want and tell people what you desire. Your true friends and people who care for you will revel in

125

your pleasure with you. These friends will also allow you to feel all of your feelings instead of insisting that you cheer up to make them more comfortable. Your truest supporters are not inconvenienced or intimidated by your multitudes. If this does not describe the people in your life, then this is your pussy's way of letting you know these are not your people.

After you have determined your self-care practices and started to tap into your pussy power, check in with your Pressure Points to see if anything has changed from the beginning of your journey or from the last time you checked in.

## Pleasure Principles:

- Once you have cleared space that once held negativity, it is important to then refill that space with positivity. You can do this through pursuing pleasure.
- Pleasure can be found even in seemingly negative emotions. Ride the wave of your emotions in the ways that feel best to you.
- Your menstrual cycle or spiritual "moon time" is the time that you are most sensitive to divine guidance.
- Through pleasure, you find flow. In flow, all things are easy and pleasurable.
- Establishing pleasurable self-care rituals is essential to developing your personal power.

Pussy Prayers

# Better Sex

**CHAPTER FIVE**

**V**
**Better Sex**

While this book is mostly about you
and your own connection to your pussy,
you will more than likely find yourself
sharing your pussy with another person at
some point in your life. It is important to
maintain the same principles even when
you are partnered.

When someone is attracted to you, it
can be attributed to the energy you are
putting forth. When we choose to partner,

we choose people who we are mutually attracted to. Individual energies recognize each other and desire to merge and expand. It is important to remember that if you are not fully standing in your feminine power, if you still deal with many insecurities or have not been taught your invaluable worth, you may attract and become attached to energies that have not come to stay forever but have come to break you open and heal you so that you are prepared for your long-term partner.

On the other side of this, you being exactly who you are supposed to be will attract people in need of what you have. Your kindness may attract mean-spirited people. Your loyalty may attract people who are duplicitous. Some ideologies will make you think that your "vibration" attracts awful people to you so you must be an awful person. This is wholly untrue. Contrary to popular belief, these people are not reflections of who you are, but proof that you have attributes and skills that the world needs. Do not allow people to take advantage of these gifts. They are yours to give, and no one (not family, not lovers, not anyone) is entitled to them.

You do not, under any circumstances, deserve, nor should you tolerate, any sort of violence or mistreatment, regardless of where you are on your path to healing. Nothing that you have experienced is your fault. You are not to blame for any negative experiences thrust upon you by another. Let this be your reminder that your pleasure is your greatest guide and indicator of the greatness and sweetness of life that the Divine has designed for you. The further you get from that, the more you choose to ignore what is unpleasant or downright terrifying, the harder it may become to find your way back to center. Be gentle with yourself. You are always learning. Be firm with others about your expectations and what you will and will not accept from them.

Do not be afraid to let people go their own way if they refuse to treat you the way you deserve to be treated. No one is worth the sacrifice of your safety, your wellbeing, your peace, or your pleasure. You may make mistakes and forget things you thought you knew. Your lessons may not take a form that you recognize. Be accountable for your actions. Forgive yourself. Be sure that if your energies are aligned with another person, you understand the purpose of the relationship and that it feels good – all ways, always.

Pussy Prayers

We are not meant to give everything
up and give all of ourselves away to a
partner. When we are trying to remain
aligned with a person and not with our
pleasure, we end up stifling ourselves and
struggling to stay connected. We think
that we have to sacrifice ourselves for
someone else's pleasure. That is false and
that does not increase our power. A divine
relationship should amplify your pleasure
and power, not diminish it. Because you
are connected to your pleasure and
committed to self-care, your juju is on and
popping before a partner even comes into
the picture. Thus, any pleasure that comes
from your partner is only an
enhancement. We cannot expect to be
refilled and refueled with a partner. A
relationship is not going to suddenly make
all of our dreams come true. Nothing

outside of yourself can bring forth your
desires and hoping that another person
does that for you is a gamble at best and a
tragedy at worst.

Pursuing your pleasure and standing in
your power will lead you to the most
fulfilling relationships, even if they don't
look the way you expected. Feel free
enough to let your relationships operate in
the way that is most pleasurable to you,
regardless of societal norms. Allow these
desires to change as they will and adjust
accordingly. Trust that as your desires
change, your environment will
accommodate to your pleasure. Do not be
afraid to release what no longer pleases
you.

**Relationship Pleasure**

You may decide that being monogamous does not bring you pleasure. You may decide that you do not want a committed relationship, but to engage romantically and sexually with an individual when you feel like it. There are no limits on the ways in which your pleasure can express itself with another person or people.

It is within your right to choose the way that you engage with others. However, being led by your pleasure does not mean that you ignore the wellbeing and consent of the people in your life. While your pleasure is priority, it is only right to allow another person's pleasure to be their priority as well. When you all no longer align or can no longer find middle ground, be okay with letting each other go in search of what feels best to you. Allow people the option of choosing to go on your journey with you or going their own way. Take into account any expectations or agreements that were formerly pleasurable to accept and adhere to. If that is no longer the case, speak up. Even if you fear an impending separation from someone you love or feel deep attachments to, trust that you are on a path to your highest good, and anyone or anything that is meant to be with you on that path will be there. Anyone or anything that is not meant to be will fall away. Trust your pussy — she won't lead you astray.

Being led by your pleasure does not mean that you disregard the pleasure of any partner or lover that you engage with.

Part of your pleasure should be honoring
your partner and their pleasure as well as
your own. As you engage with a partner
sexually, let go of your ideas of what sex is
supposed to be, what it is supposed to
look like, how long it is supposed to last,
etc. The only person that should
determine what your sex should be like is
you.

## Learn Yourself First

The first step in preparing to own
your pleasure in partnered sexual
encounters is to make sure that you know
what pleases you. You cannot expect for
your partner to come to you already
knowing the best ways to please you. Each
new partner must be schooled in the study
of your body and your pleasure, which

means you must be the expert on your body and prepared to teach someone the ins and outs of you well before engaging sexually with another person. The best way to make sure you know what you like and dislike is to explore on your own.

If we are not intimate with ourselves, we can never be truly intimate with another person. Touch your body. Can you name all the parts of your pussy? Learn what your body looks like, where things are, and what they feel like. Get to know and appreciate your scent and even your flavor. Explore your body and notice sensations in different parts of you. Notice what brings you immense pleasure and what does nothing for you. Do not limit yourself by believing what you should or should not enjoy. Don't force anything. Believe what your body tells

you. There is no such thing as normal.
Your body is yours. Your body, including
your pussy, are fine just the way they are.
What you like is what you like. As long as
you are not in pain, your body is formed
and operating as it should be. The things
that arouse you and bring you pleasure are
yours to be celebrated and practiced as
often as possible (as long as you aren't
harming yourself or anyone else).

Notice any emotional changes you feel
as you stimulate different parts of your
body. Get to the bottom of these feelings.
Are they positive or negative? Are they
blissful or shameful? Working through
these emotions is important, so do not
skip over this if it comes up for you. If
you have been affected by sexual violence
and have disassociated from your body,
especially your pussy, you may feel anxiety

or tension during these exercises. This is a
time to get reacquainted. If it is too
overwhelming or triggering in some way,
remember that getting professional help is
always an option and helpful on your
journey.

Mirror work can help you process
distance or discomfort with
acknowledging and exploring your body.
Sitting in front of a full-length mirror,
look at your body. Recall your power and
your right to pleasure back to you. Ask to
be shown what you need to see and do in
order to restore your power back to you
so that you can truly heal and return to
pleasure. Intend to return negativity and
shame to the person it belongs to. This
energy does not belong to you. It is not
yours to hold.

## On Orgasm

As you learn yourself, you should also learn what brings you to orgasm.

Orgasm is our birthright. It is what our pussies are designed to do. Learning your body helps you to learn what brings you to orgasm so that you can explain it to a partner and they can bring you to a place of overwhelming pleasure. If you feel that you have trouble reaching orgasm on your own or with a partner, do not seek the orgasm as the goal. Instead, seek the best feeling touch and sensation, and try to stay in that pleasure as long as possible. Relax into your body and trust it to perform the way it was meant to perform.

Orgasm does not have to be the expected end of every woman's sexual experience like it is for men. We have not been taught correctly about the ways in which men and women operate differently when it comes to sexuality. We have learned that something must be wrong with us if we don't reach orgasm after sex, or if we don't have multiple orgasms, or if we don't squirt. These unrealistic expectations stem from the pervasiveness of fantastical pornography and lack of comprehensive sexuality education. The pressure to "perform" during sex is what leads many women to feeling ashamed of their bodies and its function, faking orgasms to save face, and wanting to avoid sex altogether.

Clitoral stimulation is how women most often reach orgasm and most women rarely, if ever, experience orgasm simply from penetration. If you are feeling stuck or find yourself worrying about why you can't seem to orgasm instead of enjoying the sensation, return to your pussy prayer practice, laying hands on your pussy and communicating with her. See what she has to say to you. Ask her what you can do for her. Maintain confidence in your natural ability as you engage with yourself or with a partner. Trust your body and do not set out toward any goal other than simply feeling good.

Overall, orgasm is a brain function more than a pussy function. Consider your emotional state when trying to reach orgasm. Are you stressed? Are you rushed? Are there competing priorities on your mind? Are you criticizing yourself or your body in the moment? What is your environment like? Are you comfortable? Are you nervous? Afraid of getting caught? Afraid you won't perform the way you want to? All these things can distract your brain from the goal of orgasm. Stress reduces sexual interest and pleasure in virtually everyone. For most people, it is easiest to reach the peak of pleasure in a low stress, affectionate, and erotic situation. Be intentional about creating the space you need to be as relaxed as possible but remember that there is no such thing as normal. Your body is yours and operates exactly as it should.

If you are a survivor of sexual trauma and are actively working through it with professional treatment, your brain may still attach a threat or danger response in sexual situations. Be patient with yourself and keep practicing spiritual and emotional processes to help you detach the trauma from your healthy sex practices.

No matter where you start your journey, accept yourself where you are and give your body permission to do what it naturally does. The less criticizing, worrying, and thinking you can do in sexual situations, the more pleasure you allow yourself to feel.

## Partners in Sex

Sex should happen in true intimacy, honesty, and trust, as it can be medicine or poison. The best exchanges should be full of pleasure. If you do not feel safe, you will manifest symptoms of danger, your brain will go into stress mode, and you probably won't feel as good as you should during the sexual encounter. Be

discerning in where, why, and with whom
you choose to have sex.

Some people believe that casual sex is
wrong or immoral, and some believe that
it is a natural part of having a healthy sex
life. You won't find any judgments on that
here but be aware of what you're doing
and why you're doing it. If you are
engaging in sexual behaviors from a
negative or unhealthy mental and
emotional space or using sex as an escape
from internal pain, back up a little bit and
figure out how to solve the root of the
thing causing you stress so that you can
move forward in true pleasure.

Before healthy sexual encounters,
affirm that sex will be healing and
pleasurable. Repeat it to yourself and feel
it in your body. Believe that you are in
control of your pleasure and that your

partner simply amplifies that pleasure. In return, you should learn and take pride in providing pleasure for your partner. Cultivate your sexual ability and repertoire for your own and your partner's ultimate experience. It should please you to be of service to your partner, both within and outside of the realm of sex, and vice versa. Ask them what they need and how you can provide it. This is a divine privilege to manifest for the highest good of others.

## Better Sex

You may feel like sex with your partner could be better, and maybe you can't quite put your finger on what needs to change. Sex should feel good (unless you're into pain, in which case — do you, boo) and it should be fun. Sex with a partner shouldn't feel serious, like a job or an important meeting. You should be able to laugh, joke, or talk about whatever is on either of your minds. This level of healthy communication allows you to guide each other towards what you both enjoy. This is a major key in prioritizing pleasure.

If you can't talk about sex, you probably shouldn't be having it. Figure out what's making you feel unable to talk to your partner about your bodies and your desires and work through that but understand that sex can't be better until you speak up. You can't expect your partner to read your mind. Living in a sex-negative and often sexually violent society, many of us have internalized embarrassment, repulsion, avoidance, or even disgust around topics of sex. This will take time to unlearn and will improve your sex life significantly when you can talk to your partner and tell them your desires.

Sex conversations may feel awkward at first. You don't want your partner (or yourself) to feel inadequate or like an unfulfilling partner. Sensitively broach conversations (which is why fun and laughter is important) that you want to have about what you like and what you want to try. Ask your partner if there is anything that they would like that you all haven't been doing. It is best to have these conversations when you are not in a sexual situation so that you can think clearly and not feel pressured to perform immediately. There are resources in Part Two of this book to help you have these conversations.

If having fulfilling sex with your partner is important to you, then prioritize the actions that will help you get there. Do research. Read books and articles. Watch videos. Take classes. Don't be afraid to try new things together as a way to figure out what you both like. Keeping things exciting in the bedroom shouldn't be a task, but more like a fun activity that benefits you both. Shake things up every now and then with new positions, toys, environments, etc.

Be sure to manage your expectations of yourself and your partner. Maybe you've had a past partner who you had amazing sex with. It is unfair to compare your current partner to them. Your partner should not compare you to anyone from their past either. Neither of you should be held to some standard you can't possibly meet. The best thing to do for a healthy relationship (sexual, romantic, or otherwise) is figure out what works for the both of you and strive to perfect that. Remember to be patient. It takes time to learn each other, and the sex may not be making you see fireworks right away.

While you're giving it time to get better, you don't have to sacrifice your pleasure. Aside from self-pleasure sessions as you see fit, an essential part of sex is a set of pre-sex activities that we usually call foreplay. Foreplay is important because it gets you warmed up, turned on, lubricated enough for penetrative acts (if that's what you enjoy) or otherwise sensually heightened to the point where sex is desired, easy and pleasurable, putting you that much closer to orgasm. Some lazy or unknowing lovers may think that foreplay is just a little kissing, touching, rubbing, maybe licking of a nipple or two right before engaging in whatever type of penetration you prefer. For many of us, that is not nearly enough. Don't let things start before you're ready. If you're experiencing pain or discomfort when your partner attempts to put a penis, toy, or finger inside your vagina, tell them to stop. Let your partner know what you need. Direct them back to an action that makes you wetter and better prepared for action. If you find that you still aren't as wet as you'd like to be, or that it's causing you discomfort, don't be ashamed of using lubricants. Water-based or silicone-based lubricants with natural ingredients are best, and when placed in and around your vagina as well as on the penetrating toy or body part, you should find that there is more ease from discomfort caused by friction and things are more pleasurable for you both.

On the flip side of this, many times our bodies and our brains may not be giving the same signals during sex. That is to say, your brain may be ready for sex, but your pussy may not be as wet as you expect. You or your partner may not be able to tell if you're warmed up enough. There is nothing wrong with you. You are not dysfunctional. In most women, there is only a ten percent connection between the physical feeling of being "turned on" and the mental acknowledgement of being ready for sex. This just means that there are other physical cues that you and your partner can look to as signs that you're ready for sex.

You or your partner can pay attention to your breathing. When you are aroused, your breathing and pulse increase. You may also notice yourself holding your breath more as your muscles contract. Your body may become tense in areas like your wrists, abdomen, calves, buttocks, thighs, and feet to signal arousal. More than anything, you or your partner should listen for the things that you say: asking for more, affirmative language ("yes," "I love it," "I want it," etc.) and moans or other sound effects can signal how you feel.

## Don't Get Checked

Before I made a conscious effort to develop positive communication skills, I was the queen of the silent treatment. If I didn't like something, I never said anything, I just got quiet. Sometimes for a day or two. Sometimes forever. Silent treatment and avoidance of important conversations was a regular occurrence in my childhood home. People just didn't talk. They sulked. They talked shit to other people about whatever was going on. But they never actually communicated with the person that had offended them in order to solve the problem. Somehow, the other person involved was just supposed to know why a person was mad and fix it. Usually, this type of extreme resentment and suppression of feelings and desires exploded at the most inconvenient and unrelated moments, leading to many instances of violence and champion shouting matches.

Unfortunately, I carried this bad habit into my early adult years. I had to be "checked," told about myself, read up and down, before I realized that this habit was not okay. I was dating a gorgeous, intelligent, and accomplished older woman at the time. I do not remember the offense, but I remember that something I thought she had said or done had upset me. With my poor home training, I ghosted her, completely cutting off communication without explanation. This lasted for the better part of a year. In that time of no communication between she and I, I learned some new information that made me realize that I was upset over a misunderstanding, and that had I just said what I wanted or needed, or expressed my concerns about whatever the issue had been, we could still be going strong. So, trying to be the grown up I thought I was, I humbled myself and called her. In her graciousness, she invited me to lunch so we could talk in person. My life changed at that lunch because it was here that she checked me on my poor behavior. With all the kindness and understanding that I didn't deserve, she calmly explained to me that the silent treatment was not how she intended to operate in any of her personal relationships. She told me that she knew I could be more mature than I had behaved and she was disappointed that I had not voiced my concerns so she could have easily soothed my discomfort. Finally, she let me know that I needed to use my words and let her know what was going on, what I needed and wanted from her, or she would have no choice but to end communication with me because she deserved better. I ate and listened without speaking, thoroughly embarrassed by the sweetest scolding I had ever received. We were silent for what seemed like twenty minutes. I apologized softly and promised to do better.

All of this to say, can you imagine the things that could change if you just communicated effectively with your partner? Can you imagine how less stressed, anxious, or irritated you might be if you allowed a person the grace and space to make changes before deciding for them that they aren't worth the trouble? Better sex, better relationships, and better communication make the perfect combination for consistent and long-lasting love and pleasure. Don't wait until you have to get checked to make changes. Make your desires known and allow your partner to rise to meet them.

**Last Note**

This book is intentionally inclusive of all types of partnerships. However, this is particularly true if you are in or are seeking partnership with men, though this could be the case for any gender.

When you are in the middle of healing, there may be many things that your partner will not understand if they are not taking similar steps to improve their physical, emotional, and spiritual wellbeing. Do not expect them to know about you, your body, and your unique feminine experience. Do not look to them to validate or "allow" whatever it is you need to do for your highest good. Your partner should support you, love you, and respect you enough to let you do what you need to do to better yourself. If they cannot do that, they don't belong in your life.

A healthy partnership is founded on healthy communication and mutual support. If you choose to share your journey with your partner, I encourage you to explain what you are doing as best as you can and then explicitly state your expectations of them through this process. If you need them to be there for you, tell them when, where, and how. If you want them to leave you to it, let them know what that looks like. If they are a good partner, they will do their best to meet your expectations. Allow them, in good faith, to do their best and help them to refine their words and actions as necessary. Remember: there is no shortage of good partners on this planet, regardless of what your current environment might reflect. If your partner is consistently disrespectful or anything less than understanding, uplifting, and supportive, please let them go.

**Pleasure Principles:**

- You must be intimate with yourself before you can truly be intimate with anyone else. This means learning your body and what you enjoy.
- Be discerning in who you sexually engage with and communicate your desires clearly.
- You get to choose the way your relationships operate. When it is no longer pleasurable, walk away.
- The only role partners should play in your journey to healing and pleasure is one of support and love. If they can't do that, move on from them.

Pussy Prayers

Next steps

## CHAPTER SIX

165

## VI
## Next Steps

It is my prayer that this book helps you to revitalize the relationship you have with your pussy and start you down the path of never-ending pleasure. I hope that this book sparks conversation amongst girlfriends and sister circles, making it commonplace to discuss sexuality, emotions, desires, and anything else. Remember that it is your divine responsibility to care for yourself, honor yourself, step into your power, and allow pleasure to fill every aspect of your life. I hope that after reading this, you can step forward in this realm as a model of unapologetic divine femininity and have the confidence to be a sacred space in a world that does not believe that women should have such power

History has taught us shame and to find fault with our bodies. As we unlearn and relearn, we must pass our knowledge along to other women. Use this book to heal yourself, then pass it down to your daughter, your sister, your niece, your cousin, or any other young women in your life as they journey to and through womanhood. Help to break the generational curses and traumas to build up confident young women who have healthy relationships with their bodies and know how to heal themselves. Now that you know how to write a new story and create a new reality, I challenge you to create a *new* history so that when your great-granddaughters describe the ways in which they came into their womanhood, they describe an empowering, sacred, joyful experience. May you and your maternal lineage always be beacons of love and divinity and always remember how to manifest your highest and deepest desires.

I hope that you see your womanhood differently after reading this book. I hope that you found resonance, relief, and much-needed laughter around topics that can often be heavy, traumatic, or depressing. Remember, we are sisters, creators, magical juju mamas entitled to —

literally wired for – pleasure, acceptance, forgiveness, stability, discernment, safety, confidence, clarity, connection, truth, freedom, and more. These are yours, gifted to you through your divinity. You are healing from the center.

You found and read this book for a reason. If you did not believe it before, I hope that you understand that nothing you have experienced has negated your holiness, that everything you seek is within you, and that you are gracefully and divinely learning how to feel deeply, heal, and curate and cultivate pleasure in every aspect of your life.

The next section of this book lays out resources and activities to guide you along your journey. Remember, this book is an introduction, not an encyclopedia. Think of this book as your first stepping stone on a lifelong path to fully realized divine femininity. As you move through this work, pay attention to the teachers and more advanced resources that show up. Healing can come from all kinds of people, places, and things. Stay alert. If there is a subject mentioned here that you would like to know more about, do your research. Ask for divine guidance on the information you seek. Trust that you will receive exactly what you need, exactly when you need it.

**Thank you for reading!**

If you enjoyed this book, it would be awesome if you could share a quick review on Amazon or whatever platform you purchased this book from. You can also send reviews to

**hello@blackgirlbliss.com** to help other women make the decision to take back control of their power and get back in touch with their pussies.

If you know someone who is struggling with their sexuality, spirituality, or self-care, please send them a copy of this book.

If you want to go deeper into the ideas and activities outlined here, I invite you to explore the additional resources on the website (I couldn't include every single thing in this text because we'd be here forever).

If you feel like you need a teacher or coach to go through this process with you, holding your hand every step of the way and creating a plan for you to get the healing and pleasure you deserve, there are services available. Visit

Pussy Prayers

**BlackGirlBliss.com** for more
information.

PART TWO

Pressure Points

CHAPTER SEVEN

# VII
## Pressure Points

Journaling is an important part of your journey to healing and pleasure. Make time to reflect and preserve your learning and growth along this journey.

The following pages are additional *Pressure Points* that you can use as journal prompts. Remember that these questions may evoke emotional responses depending on where you are in your journey. Allow those emotions to come and record them so that you can chart your growth through the process.

1. Who taught you about what it meant to be a woman? When did you learn it and how did it make you feel about womanhood?
2. What is "feminine" in your own words? Do you feel feminine? Why or why not?
3. Do you enjoy being a woman? Have you always enjoyed womanhood? Explain.
4. Is there a presence of divine femininity in your life, whether through your own personal spiritual practice or an organized religion? How does this feminine presence (or lack thereof)

influence your ideas of femininity and womanhood?

5. Name your pleasures. All of them. Even the ones that sound or feel silly.

6. What do you think your pussy would like to discuss with you?

7. In what ways have you ignored your pussy, past or present?

8. When or with whom has it been most difficult to be yourself or speak your truth?

9. What have you used to cope or ignore pain related to your sexuality or womanhood?

10. What has happened in your life that has negatively or positively affected your pussy or your relationship with her?

11. Tell the story of the first time you saw and/or interacted with your pussy. If you have never done so, express why you haven't.
12. What are your current feelings about your pussy? Are they positive or negative?
13. How did you develop the feelings you have about your pussy? Do you want to change these feelings or enhance them? How do you plan to do so?
14. What pain can you identify surrounding your pussy or your womanhood in general that you experienced from childhood to present? Where did this pain come from?
15. Consider your sexual orientation. How would you define yourself?

Why do you define yourself this way?

16. Have you ever been embarrassed, punished, or scolded for displays of sexuality? Tell what happened and how that has affected you.

17. Think of your past lovers or lovers you would have liked to have. Ask your pussy how she feels about them. Record what comes up for each person.

18. Have you been pregnant? Have you had abortions? Have you given birth? How many times? How has this affected your relationship to your pussy?

19. Write out all the words that come to mind when you think about sex. Then look at those words and

think about what they reveal about your feelings about sex.

20. Describe your first menstrual cycle. Was it positive or negative? Who supported and educated you on your body? What did they say? What do you wish this experience would have been like?

21. Tell the story of your first sexual experience. Make a list of all the sexual experiences you've ever had. Reflect on the feelings that come up. How has this affected your relationship with your pussy and your understanding of sexuality and womanhood?

22. Consider your past and present relationships. How do these relationships make you feel about your pussy?

23. Are there things that you will not allow your lover to do to you? Why is that?
24. Are there things that you secretly wish your lover would do to you, with you, or for you? What are these things? Have you told your current partner these things?
25. Confront any history of sexual abuse you have experienced. How have these experiences shaped your ideas of sexuality and womanhood?
26. Of the following issues, which of these do you have? When did they begin? How have you tried to heal them? Record and return to this list to record any improvements.

- Absent menstrual cycle
- Irregular menstrual cycle
- Long menstrual cycle
- Menopausal symptoms
- Intense menstrual cramps
- Mood swings/PMS
- Vaginal itching or burning
- Strong vaginal odor
- Cysts (internal or external)
- Vaginitis or vaginosis
- Painful penetration
- Inability to orgasm
- Sexually transmitted infections
- Infertility
- Vaginal dryness
- Fibroids/tumors
- Endometriosis

## Pussy Prayers

- _____

- _____

- _____

# pussy prayers:

## AFFIRMATIONS, MEDITATIONS, AND RITUALS

## CHAPTER EIGHT

# VIII
## Pussy Prayers:
## Affirmations, Meditations, and Rituals

This chapter outlines various practices for you to establish and maintain a relationship with your pussy. Remember that consistency and intention are most important when establishing these practices. Make them a regular part of your self-care practice. If there is anything that comes up for you that is overwhelming or causes you significant emotional pain, please reach out to a trusted advisor or professional therapist.

## Rituals

Rituals are a combination of action and intention. It is a method through which you invite the Divine into a space to assist in the transformation of energy. Recognizing and acting on your power to get what you need from the Universe is realized through ritual. Ideas for rituals are listed first here so that you understand the context in which to use the following meditations, affirmations, and other resources. Feel free to modify or reimagine these rituals in ways that are

185

more meaningful to you. Remember, consistency and intention are key.

## Pussy Altar

Think about how you could create a space to honor your pussy, the Divine Feminine, and your own ideal experience of womanhood. It can be as big or as small as you'd like, out in the open or somewhere only you will ever see. Don't worry so much about getting it "right" but focus on how it makes you feel. This is a space for you to connect with you. Use your imagination and create with colors, textures, and objects that resonate with you. If you get the seemingly random idea to do something with your space, go with it.

You might find yourself at a loss for ideas, and that's okay too. Be patient with the way this space comes together. Set the intention to create a space to commune and connect with your pussy, the center of your power, and your Divine Feminine, then watch how things align to lead you to the exact things you want.

Some items you might want to add to this space are incense, candles, crystals, photos, quotes, affirmations, female figurines or other representations of the feminine, female-centered art, a special journal and pen, books, fabric, pillows, and a mat for movement activities.

Once you create your space, decide what you will do there. You can meditate, journal, pray, sing, dance, do yoga, talk out loud, or anything else that feels good to you. Set a routine for yourself that works for your energy and your schedule. Keep the space clean and beautiful. Change it as often as you choose to.

## Vaginal Steaming

Water is a necessity and a game changer not just for physical health, but for spiritual and emotional reasons as well. We are water. All things that have an effect on water also have an effect on us. Healing baths, herbal teas, vaginal steams, and spiritual ceremonies near water tend to have a profound cleansing effect on our bodies and our spirits. For our pussy's purposes here, vaginal steaming is described as an option to add to your self-care practice.

Vaginal steaming (also known as "v-steaming," "yoni steaming," or "womb saunas") infuses the herbal and spiritual properties of certain plants for the purpose of healing physical and spiritual vaginal and sex-related issues. This is an ancient practice that spans countries and cultures. Vaginal steaming is not the same as douching and is not necessarily for the purpose of "cleaning" the vagina (the vagina needs no help getting clean). The process of vaginal steaming involves sitting over a pot of herb-infused water for a short period of time. Vaginal steaming has been known to help heal issues such as infertility, fibroids, ovarian cysts, PCOS, pelvic pain, irregular menstruation, and endometriosis, as well as help women heal post-pregnancy. This should not replace traditional medicine, so if you live with these medical issues be sure to seek appropriate treatment in addition to beginning this practice. This practice is still effective for women who do not menstruate or who have had hysterectomies or other removal of reproductive parts as it can stimulate healthy circulation, soothe any inflammation, and help tone the muscles of the entire pelvic region.

You should pick up to five herbs for your steam based on their properties (there is a list of suitable herbs for vaginal steaming in the next chapter.) You will need about a cup of dried herbs for a large pot of water. Make sure the herbs that you use come from a reputable store or source so that you are getting the expected benefit. Do not use essential oils for vaginal steaming as these are concentrated and can cause irritation, burns, or other serious issues to the sensitive skin in the vulvovaginal area.

After you choose your formula of herbs specific to your purpose, begin by saying a prayer of thanks to the plants for their aid in your efforts, and set your intentions for what you want to happen during this steam. Affirm your healing from the beginning to the end of this process. Place your herbs in a pot of filtered or distilled water and let them simmer on low to medium heat for ten to twenty minutes. Do this in the mindset of making tea as opposed to boiling collard greens. You are not trying to cook the herbs, but simply infuse them into the water. Do not allow the water to boil or it will be too hot for you to comfortably use. You're about to sit your bare pussy over this water; you don't want to burn yourself! When finished, the water should have a steady, opaque steam. Test the water on your forearm or hold your palm over the steam to make sure you won't burn yourself. It should be hot but not painful. Pour the steamed herbs into a heat-safe bowl and bring it to your steaming space.

Setting up your steam space can be as luxurious or simple as time, privacy, and your desire allows. Assuming you do not have a special vaginal steaming seat (available at various retailers online), you can use a slotted chair, a step stool with a slot in the middle, or place the bowl of steaming herbs inside your (clean!) toilet and sit on the toilet seat. Whatever your choice, make sure that when you place your bowl underneath you, you can feel the steam on your pussy, as close to the perineum area (between your vagina and anus) as possible, without burning yourself. You should be completely naked at least from the waist down. Have a blanket or towel to wrap around you that extends to the floor while you sit to keep you warm and keep the steam in. Sweating during this process is ideal. As you sit on your seat, wrapped, with the steam underneath you, you want to maintain a relaxed atmosphere. Play music, light candles, burn incense, bring water or tea for your comfort, read a book, or simply sit in silence for twenty to thirty minutes. Breathe deeply to help your muscles relax. If you choose, you can even hold healing crystals that match your intentions in your hands as you steam and meditate. Some ideas for the types of crystals to use are in the next chapter.

Pussy Prayers

As you sit over the steam, you may
feel the urge to pee, but it will go away
(pee before you begin, just in case). Your
pussy may release discharge, mucus, old
uterine tissue or blood, and it's not
unheard of to release parasites if you have
them. Do not be alarmed as these are
extreme cases. More often than not, you
won't be able to feel or tell that anything
has come out of you. After steaming, dry
off, shower if you wish, put on warm
clothes, and lie down under a blanket to
keep your body relaxed. Your pussy may
continue to release fluids post-steam so
you may want to wear a pad or panty liner.

You may see your menstrual cycle
come early after you've steamed. You may
also notice with your next menstrual cycle
that you release darker blood, or more
tissue and clots than normal. This is a

positive sign since you want to release old blood and tissue that has just been sitting in your uterus. The following cycles may feature bright red, "fresh" blood, which is a sign that everything is working as it should.

Vaginal steams can be done as frequently as twice per week (for cysts, pain, etc.) or as infrequently as once per season (for maintenance and regular cleansing), depending on your needs. Steaming should not happen while you are menstruating or while having an active episode of any infection or condition that causes rash, open wounds, or broken skin as the sweat may irritate or spread the issue. Hold off on vaginal steaming if you are pregnant until six to eight weeks after you have given birth to ensure you are not bleeding and there is no infection. If you have had a miscarriage or abortion, wait three weeks to ensure there is no infection or other serious complications. If you have been trying to conceive, do not steam during or after ovulation. If you have an intrauterine device (IUD) for birth control, vaginal steaming may soften the cervix enough to displace the device.

Baths and steaming are a form of holistic health treatment and intimate self-care, so take your time, make it personal, and be consistent with your practice.

## Temple Care Contract

Write up a sacred contract between you and your pussy. Make an agreement with yourself on how you will treat yourself and how you will allow others to treat you. List out all of the ways that you are committing to caring for yourself and making sure that you are experiencing as much #EverydayDeliciousness as possible. Writing it by hand will make this a more intimate experience. Use your very best handwriting, draw pictures, use colors, whatever feels good to you. You can put this in a private place or hang it up somewhere that you will always be able to see. Try your best to stick to it, and when you fall off (because we all fall off, sometimes) forgive yourself, extend yourself grace, and hop right back in there.

## Sister Circle

Having a sister circle can be one of the most healing experiences you can have. This is a group of women who are committed to holding space and bearing witness to each other's growth. This is a safe space where everyone is committed to not only their own healing and pleasure but the healing and pleasure of everyone in the circle. You should hold each other accountable, lift each other up, comfort each other in times of pain, and celebrate the wins of all as if they were your own. This circle can be made up of all kinds of women and can be a profound intergenerational experience. This can be an educational space for all women involved, because how often do we get time to just sit and talk about ourselves and our bodies? Healing collectively creates positive momentum for everyone and is a bonding experience for women of all relations and walks of life. This is a group that you can tell your secrets to and know that they will be kept. In this space you can have discussions, prayer, meditation, singing, dancing, activities, or anything else the group agrees to.

Up to ten people can agree to meet once per week, every other week, or once per month, and you can take turns hosting at each other's homes. Each person in the group should have their own personal goals for healing and pleasure. You all should commit to the work set forth by this book and by your unique collective needs. Set your collective intention for the space. Make it a pleasurable affair, one that everyone looks forward to in order to keep the energy high and the commitment solid. Prepare the atmosphere with scents, soft lights, and music. Decide on a regular order of events for each meeting. Keep up with each other. Allow each person to share their wins and challenges. Above all, care for each other, love each other, and help each other heal.

## Creative Expression and Adornment

Connection with your pussy will draw out many creative pursuits and ideas, ones that you may not have even known you could do. Let yourself be guided to create the things that bring you pleasure. Do not feel pressured to create the greatest thing that has ever existed, or even to share your creations. Your pussy is the portal through which all things are manifested and brought to this realm. If you have trouble with creative blocks, you might need to have a word with your pussy.

Adorning yourself is a means of creativity as well. Ask your pussy what she feels good in, what feels good to put on. From lotions to scents to jewelry to clothing, what you put on your body is a testament to your connection with yourself. The better you feel, the more connected you are.

## Pussy Talks

All women are intuitive. At our core, we know all we need to know. The only thing that changes is the ways in which we receive intuitive messages. Almost always, we receive messages through our senses. We see, hear, smell, taste, touch, or feel when something is positive or negative, when we should act and when we shouldn't, if the people around us are in trouble or up to no good, and many other pieces of intel that keep us safe and guide our path. If you're listening for some foreign voice to speak into your head like a radio, change your expectation.

We have to learn our pussy's language. How does she communicate to you? Physical sensations in a certain part of your body? Thoughts that seem to come from someone outside of yourself? Dreams or visions that might be literal foreshadowing or symbolic representation of things to come? Pay attention to these things and other ways of "knowing" that happen to you. Messages may not come right away but keep at it. If you have trouble receiving these messages or feel like you aren't that in tune with your intuition, you need to reconnect with your pussy. Keep record of your pussy talks in a journal or somewhere you can access at a later time to reflect on your progress of connecting with your pussy and clearly hearing what she has to say.

## Food and Movement

You may not want to hear this, but the food you eat and your level of physical activity has a major effect on the state of your pussy and your connection to her. Food is a sacred and sensual choice, and what you eat changes you. You may notice that PMS and other vaginal and reproductive issues can be made worse by the things you eat or improved by increase exercise or activity.

Dairy, sugar, meat, wheat, and alcohol are typically the main culprits in pelvic discomfort or issues. For a healthy, happy pussy, make sure you are eating fresh fruits and vegetables daily. This is not a command to go vegan. I cannot presume to tell you what and how to eat. I am telling you to be mindful and intentional. There is a list of foods that are beneficial to your vaginal health in the Resources section. If you choose to eat meat, remember that something gave up its life for you. Your body will change and use this body for the highest good. Preparing meals at home can be a pleasurable ritual and can ensure that you know exactly what you are putting into your body. Show your gratitude for all food you consume and set the intention that it will be nourishing and beneficial to your body.

Try to drink at least forty ounces of water per day. (That's a little more than two standard sized bottles of water. Yes, you will pee. It won't kill you.) If you do not like the "taste" of water, that is a sign that your body is trained to desire sugary drinks that do nothing for your hydration or your health. Add fruit or herbal tea bags to your water if you desire flavor or explore the many varieties of sparkling water if you miss the carbonation of soda.

For those that are typically sedentary or have joint and muscle pain, start slowly with exercise. Begin by setting aside time to breathe deeply and stretch. Leg and abdominal stretches and exercises are great for engaging your core and getting the energy moving through the lower parts of your body. After some time, incorporate walking or jogging. Dancing, hula hooping, and other rhythmic movement will also help move energy

Pussy Prayers

through your body and can be more
pleasurable than standard exercises.

## Affirmations

Here is a list of affirmations that you can use within a ritual or whenever you need to affirm your power, your pleasure, and your healing. Feel free to modify them to fit your situation. Memorize them and say them over and over again. Post them where you will see them often or write them repeatedly as a form of meditation. Choose one or two phrases to focus on at a time to really commit them to memory and begin the mental and spiritual process of making them true for you.

Pussy Prayers

- I am worthy of pleasure.
- Pleasure is my birthright and I intend to experience it daily.
- My life is full of pleasure and ease.
- Pleasure is available to me at any time.
- I am committed to my pleasure.
- I love my pussy and my pussy loves me.
- My pussy always guides me toward pleasure.
- My pussy knows best. I trust her.
- I have made peace with my past.
- I am healed on every level.
- I release all negativity that does not belong to me.
- I am powerful in pleasure.

- My pleasure is my priority.
- I attract lovers who love me well.
- I am in control of my mind and my body.
- I am whole in every way.
- I am free of other people's expectations of my womanhood.
- I am a powerful creator and I manifest whatever I wish.
- I radiate and attract love, peace, and pleasure.
- Sex is healing and pleasurable for me.
- I am perfect.
- I am divine.
- I am delicious.
- I attract experiences that make my life juicy.

209

Pussy Prayers

- I experience more pleasure every day.
- My journey is mine and it is perfect for me.
- I find the perfect teachers to guide me on my journey.
- I am grateful for the freedom and pleasure I experience every day.
- I find pleasure in ordinary things.
- I am open to receiving delightful surprises.
- I have mastery over my mind and body.
- My life is blossoming perfectly.
- I deserve pleasure in every way.
- My body is the temple that houses my spirit and I treat it with reverence and care. I nourish my mind, body, and soul.

- The more pleasure I experience, the more power I have.
- I release drama and hardship. They are not mine to hold.
- My life is good. My life feels good.
- I communicate well, and all my needs are met.
- I can tap into pleasure whenever I wish.
- I sleep knowing that I am divinely guided and protected.
- I overflow with passion, fulfillment, and happiness.
- My relationships are fun, honest, and intimate.
- Pleasure is my natural state.
- I feel powerful in my life right now, even as I strive toward healing.

Pussy Prayers

- I know exactly what to do at every moment.
- I attract all that I need. I attract only the best.
- I am proud of myself for what I have survived.
- I accept myself as I am, and I am excited for how I intend to grow.

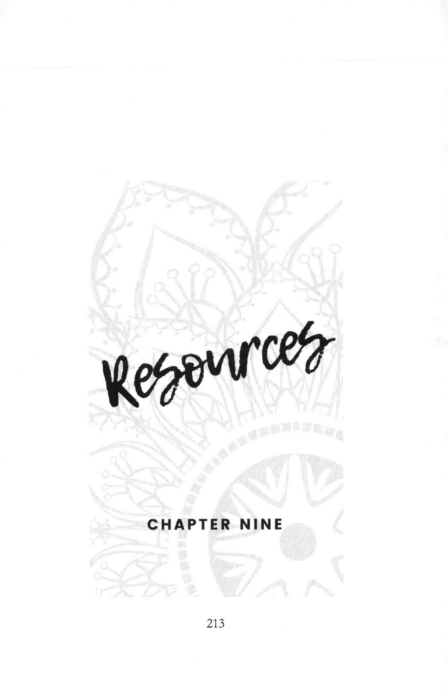

# Resources

**CHAPTER NINE**

## IX
## Resources

This chapter provides information that will help you better understand the ideas outlined in Part One of the book. You will also find activities and suggested additional readings here. Use this chapter as a reference guide on your journey to healing and pleasure.

## Pussy Positive Herbs

Listed here are herbs that are beneficial to the vagina and reproductive system. This list is not exhaustive. Remember, this book is just an introduction, a starting point, and it is your responsibility to continue your journey from here. Please do your own research before using these herbs or consult an experienced herbalist before consuming, steaming, or bathing in these herbs. Some of these herbs can be dangerous, even lethal, if prepared, measured, or consumed incorrectly. Be aware of any allergies you have that may be affected by these herbs as they are still plant matter even if they are dried. If you notice any irritation or reaction after using any of these herbs, stop immediately and

see a medical professional. These should
not take the place of any prescribed
medications or medical treatment.

- Basil
- Black Cohosh
- Calendula/Marigold
- Cinnamon
- Chamomile
- Damiana
- Dandelion
- Dong Quai
- Juniper
- Lavender
- Lemon Balm
- Maca Root
- Marshmallow Root
- Mint

- Moringa
- Motherwort
- Mugwort
- Nettle
- Nutmeg
- Oatstraw
- Oregano
- Plantain
- Red Clover
- Red Raspberry Leaf
- Red Rose Petals
- Rosemary
- Sage
- Slippery Elm
- Witch Hazel
- Yarrow

## Coochie-Comforting Crystals

Listed here are crystals whose properties align with the Divine Feminine, healing and releasing of trauma, and increasing feminine and sexual energy. This list is not exhaustive. All of these crystals can be found in egg shapes but only some of them are safe to insert into the vagina. Do your due diligence to learn about the safety of yoni eggs and which should be used for that purpose. If in doubt, simply hold them in your hands or rest them on top of any area you want to focus on. Crystals should be cleansed regularly and charged with the desired intention before each use.

- Amethyst
- Amber
- Aquamarine
- Aventurine
- Clear Quartz
- Fluorite
- Jade
- Moonstone
- Opal
- Red Carnelian
- Rhodonite
- Rose Quartz
- Smoky Quartz
- Sodalite
- Unakite

## Yummy Yoni Foods

Listed here are foods that aid in your pussy's overall wellbeing. Increasing the frequency of these foods in your diet can improve fertility, lubrication, and pH balance. These foods are not cure-alls but should be consumed in addition to your lifestyle change as you intentionally reconnect with and care for your pussy. This list is not exhaustive but should provide a starting point for this step in your journey. Do more of your own research on the vitamins and minerals your pussy needs for optimum health and which foods contain them. As a general rule, all fruits and vegetables should be staples in your diet, as well as copious amounts of water.

- Almonds
- Apple
- Avocado
- Banana
- Berries
- Broccoli
- Carrots
- Chia Seeds
- Cranberries (no added sugar)
- Cucumber
- Dark Chocolate
- Dark, Leafy Greens
- Flaxseed
- Garlic
- Ginger
- Grapefruit
- Hemp seeds
- Honeydew
- Lemon
- Lime

Pussy Prayers

- Mango
- Okra
- Olive oil
- Oranges
- Papaya
- Peaches
- Peppers
- Pineapple
- Probiotics
- Pumpkin seeds
- Quinoa
- Salmon
- Sunflower seeds
- Sweet Potato
- Walnuts
- Watermelon

## How to Talk about Sex

Having a conversation about sex can be awkward, but it doesn't have to be. Here are some tips to help you have the discussion with your partner in a way that is productive and fun.

- Channel your former high school self. Write letters to each other about what you like and what you want, complete with silly doodles and hearts with your initials in the middle.

- Have the conversation in a place that you typically wouldn't talk about such things. The pressure is off since you're not in bed at that moment, and the taboo nature of it all can be arousing.

- Make flash cards with sentence starters like: "I like…," "I don't like…" "When I'm in the mood, it looks like…," "When I'm not in the mood, it looks like…," "When I want you to keep going, I'll say…," "When I want you to stop, I'll say…," and so on. Take turns choosing a card and both of you complete the sentence out loud with whatever makes the sentence true for you.

- Share a notebook between you and your partner. Write down the things you want your partner to know and leave it where they'll know to look for it. They should then read it on their own time, away from you, and respond to what you wrote and write their own desires in the notebook. Then you will go back to it, read their writing, and respond back. This can help relieve the pressure of having to respond in the moment and give you both time to think about what you want to say.

- Explore foreplay as a way of experiencing all day arousal and pleasure, leading up to the "big event" with your partner, as opposed to just a little kiss or lick here and there before the action starts. Think of ways to tease and turn your partner on throughout the day. Keep in mind that sexual interest and pleasure is stifled by stress. What can you do to make sure you and your partner come to bed stress-free and ready to play?

## Starting a Pussy Prayers Book Club

Starting a book club with your sister circle or any other supportive and like-minded group of women can help you to work through the concepts outlined throughout this book. In this section, you will find discussion points, activities for each chapter, and suggested reading for further study. You can choose to read through the chapter together or to come to the book club session having already read. The ideas outlined here are just a starting point. Feel free to create your own discussions and activities around the concepts of the book.

## Session One: History and Context

**Reading:** Chapter 1 — "Start Here"

**Opening:** Have each person share what they hope to understand or solve by reading this book. Set the intention for the collective to receive all that they need and be led to their highest good through the collective study of this book.

### Discussion Questions:

- What word do you prefer to use to describe your vagina? Do certain words elicit a negative response from you? Why?

- Have you treated yourself like holy ground? Why or why not?

**Final Reflections:** Has anything surprised you, brought up emotions, or made you think in this chapter? Share with the group.

**Homework:** Reflect on the possible traumas the women in your family endured that affected the way that they approached or ignored topics of womanhood and sexuality.

## Session Two: Acknowledgement

**Reading:** Chapter 2 — "Attention Please"

**Opening:** What have the Pressure Points brought up for you so far? Share with the group.

## Discussion Questions:
- In what ways has your pussy been trying to get your attention and you have ignored it? Why?
- How did you come to learn about yourself and your sexuality? Was it positive or negative? Was it nonexistent?

**Final Reflections:** How have you been connected or disconnected from your pussy? How has it affected you?

**Homework:** Make a plan to begin detoxing and clearing your trauma and negativity. Write it out and figure out what steps you need to take.

Pussy Prayers

**Session Three: Action**

**Reading:** Chapter 3 — "Reclamation"

**Opening:** When did you learn about sex? Who taught you? Was it positive? Traumatic?

**Discussion Questions:**
- How have your ideas or attitudes towards womanhood and sexuality changed so far?
- How have you been tending to your temple? Do you need to make changes? How do you plan to do so?
- What is currently pleasurable in your life?

**Final Reflections:** How are you committing to the reclamation of your pussy and your feminine power?

**Homework:** Complete or review more Pressure Points from Chapter 7. Has anything changed or surprised you?

## Session Four: Praxis

**Reading:** Chapter 4 — "Everyday Deliciousness"

**Opening:** Have you fallen short on the intentions you set for yourself yet? What's going on and how have you tried to get back on track? How can the group support you?

## Discussion Questions:

- Are you afraid of letting your pleasure lead you? Why or why not?

- How has your ego shown up to derail you during this process? How did you keep going?

- What is your favorite pleasure activity or ritual? Which do you plan to try?

**Final Reflections:** How do you feel knowing that you are "allowed" to feel all of your feelings and that this, too, is a form of pleasure?

**Homework:** Complete a ritual from Chapter 8 and record your reflections on the process and your emotional state.

**Session Five: Intimacy**

**Reading:** Chapter 5 — "Better Sex" and Chapter 6 — "Next Steps"

**Opening:** Are you uncomfortable talking about sex with your partner? Why?

**Discussion Questions:**
- How have you explored your own sexual likes and dislikes?
- Does your current romantic relationship look and operate in a way that brings you both the most pleasure? What would your ideal romantic relationship look like?

**Final Reflections:** Do you have issues with being consistent? Why? What takes you off track? How can you be held accountable for being consistent? What will you be doing differently for yourself after reading this book?

**Homework:** Is the pressure to orgasm a point of frustration for you? Do you aspire to be multi-orgasmic or orgasm solely from penetration? Reflect on where this pressure to perform comes from. Who are you trying to appease or impress?

## Sources, Inspiration, Suggested Additional Reading

- **Becoming Cliterate: Why Orgasm Equality Matters — And How to Get It** by Laurie Mintz

- **Come as You Are: The Surprising New Science That Will Transform Your Sex Life** by Emily Nagoski

- **Holistic Sexuality: A Practical Guide to Sexual Healing** by K. Akua Gray

- **Living an Orgasmic Life: Heal Yourself and Awaken Your Pleasure** by Xanet Pailet

- **Love Your Lady Landscape: Trust Your Gut, Care for 'Down There', and Reclaim Your Fierce and Feminine SHE-Power** by Lisa Lister

- **Pussy: A Reclamation** by Regena Thomashauer

- **Sacred Woman: A Guide to Healing the Feminine Body, Mind, and Spirit** by Queen Afua

- **Sistah Vegan: Black Women Speak on Food, Identity, Health, and Society** by A. Breeze Harper (Chapter 19: The Food and Sex Link by Angelique Shofar)

- **Tantra: The Supreme Understanding** by OSHO

- **The Art of Everyday Ecstasy: The Seven Tantric Keys for Bringing Passion, Spirit, and Joy into Every Part of Your Life** by Margot Anand

- **The Ethical Slut: A Practical Guide to Polyamory, Open Relationships, & Other Adventures** by Janet W. Hardy

- **The Wild Woman's Way: Unlock Your Full Potential for Pleasure, Power, and Fulfillment** by Michaela Boehm

- **Urban Tantra: Sacred Sex for the Twenty-First Century** by Barbara Carrellas

- **Vagina: Revised and Updated Edition** by Naomi Wolf

Pussy Prayers

- **Wild Feminine: Finding Power, Spirit, and Joy in the Female Body** by Tami Lynn Kent

- **Women Who Run With the Wolves: Myths and Stories of the Wild Woman Archetype** by Clarissa Pinkola Estes

- **You Look Like Something Blooming: A Memoir of Divination Seeds to Cultivate Your Feminine Garden Temple** by India Ame'ye

**BLACK GIRL BLISS** is an educational
platform dedicated to cultivating the
spiritual, sexual, and self-care practices of
Black women and femmes. Learn more at
**BlackGirlBliss.com**

Made in the USA
Columbia, SC
02 September 2022

66503470R00145